THE REAL THING

Coke's Bumpy Ride through India

To my mother,
my source of inspiration

THE REAL THING

Coke's Bumpy Ride through India

Nantoo Banerjee

frontpage

frontpage
www.frontagepublications.com

First published 2009 by
frontpage

ISBN 978-81-903580-5-7

Published by frontpage
Apt # 201, Dehali, 221 Jodhpur Park, Kolkata 700068
Printed at N K Gossain & Co Private Limited
13/7 Ariff Road, Kolkata 700067
Typeset by Compuset International
85 Park Street, Kolkata 700016

This edition is published in collaboration with The Publisher, New Delhi

Contents

Acronyms and Abbreviations

ASSOCHAM	Associated Chambers of Commerce and Industry
BAT	British American Tobacco
BBD	Best Before Date
BBHL	Britannia Brand Holdings Limited
BCCNE	Bharat Coca-Cola Bottling North East Pvt. Limited
BCCSE	Bharat Coca-Cola Bottling South East Pvt. Limited
BIS	Bureau of Indian Standards
BJP	Bharatiya Janata Party
CCEA	Cabinet Committee on Economic Affairs
CCSAH	Coca-Cola South Asia Holdings Inc.
CFL	Central Food Laboratory
CFO	Chief Financial Officer
CFTRI	Central Food Technological Research Institute
CGWA	Central Ground Water Authority
CII	Confederation of Indian Industry
COBC	Code of Business Conduct
CPCB	Central Pollution Control Board
CSD	Carbonated Soft Drinks
CSE	Centre for Science and Environment
CSR	Corporate Social Responsibility
DST	Department of Science and Technology
EEC	European Economic Commission

EIA	Environment Impact Assessment
ESIA	Environment and Social Impact Assessment
FDI	Foreign Direct Investment
FICCI	Federation of Indian Chambers of Commerce and Industry
FIPB	Foreign Investment Promotion Board
FPO	Fruit Products Order
FT	Financial Times
GAP	Good Agricultural Practices
GATT	General Agreement on Tariffs and Trade
GDP	Gross Domestic Product
HCCB	Hindustan Coca-Cola Beverages Pvt. Limited
HCCH	Hindustan Coca-Cola Beverages Holdings Pvt. Limited
HCCNW	Hindustan Coca-Cola Bottling Northwest Pvt. Limited
HCCSW	Hindustan Coca-Cola Bottling Southwest Pvt. Limited
HLL	Hindustan Lever Limited
IFC	International Finance Corporation
IMF	International Monetary Fund
IPO	Initial Public Offer
IUPAC	International Union of Pure and Applied Chemistry
JPC	Joint Parliamentary Committee
KSPCB	Kerala State Pollution Control Board
MNC	Multinational Corporation
MRL	Maximum Residue Limit
NABL	National Accreditation Board for Testing and Calibration for Laboratories
NGOs	Non-Government Organizations

NRIs	Non-resident Indians
OCBs	Overseas Corporate Bodies
OPEC	Organization of Petroleum Exporting Countries
PCB	Pollution Control Board
PFA	Prevention of Food Adulteration
PTI	Press Trust of India
RAC	Raw Agricultural Commodities
SEBI	Securities and Exchange Board of India
SEC	Securities and Exchange Commission
SIBA	Standard International Bottlers Agreement
TCCC	The Coca-Cola Company
WBIDC	West Bengal Industrial Development Corporation
WEF	World Economic Forum
WSF	World Social Forum
WWF	World Wildlife Fund

Preface

After 25 years in business and financial journalism, I left the profession in February 2000 to taste life from the other side of the fence. The complexities of corporate organizations are far more intricate than what a business journalist generally pretends to know. Despite my close interaction and regular contact with industry barons, bosses of banks and financial institutions, professional managers, business and market regulators, minority shareholders, trade union leaders, opinion leaders, bureaucrats and ministers for almost three decades, the nuances of corporate management continue to be an enigma. I feel a media person's knowledge of a corporation and its management is somewhat superficial. Management is a mysterious entity. Very often, it does not know enough about itself. The body corporate is often blind to its own actions, inactions, motives and results. Nevertheless, its self-assessment rating is generally exceptional. It is not always willing to learn. When it starts, it is often too late. It tends to consider other entities and society at large to be blind. When the corporate body does not know itself well enough, how can an outsider? In large organizations, members of the key management team or function heads often operate in silos. If they could, they would prefer to either conceal or play down their functional failures rather than share the information with other colleagues in the core management team to avoid crises.

A corporation is also a legal entity. It often seeks refuge in the law when in trouble or exposed for wrongdoings. The larger the corporation, the more formidable is its clout and it feels more insulated from criticism or opposition. It often flexes its muscles to destroy dissent, internal or external. Pushed to a corner, the corporate management can even go to the extent of threatening its critics and detractors. A person can gauge the management mind only from within or by being part of the body. Such a person would rarely share inside knowledge – especially the shenanigans within the organization – with stakeholders and the public. This explains why there are so many corporate success stories in the market and so little written about the failures. The muckraking begins only after the collapse of an enterprise affecting the lives of thousands of innocent investors, creditors, suppliers and, of course, employees. In India, not even 10 per cent of the companies listed on the stock exchange are able to fulfil the expectations of the shareholders based on promises made at the time of their initial public offerings (IPOs). How many shareholders, or even their creditors, know what exactly is wrong with their companies, or why their performance failed to match their promises? How much of this can be blamed on management failure? Case studies of management failures rarely unravel the flaws of those mystery men or women at the helm, how their minds work and why they do what they do to destroy the reputation of an enterprise. I am fairly sure that the Enron management or Warren Anderson of Union Carbide were not deliberately trying to foul things up to earn the wrath of a group of regulators and law enforcers. My suspicion is that neither Rajan Pillai, nor Manohar Rajaram Chhabria, both NRI tycoons, deliberately fashioned their personal misery. Circumstances forced them into murky relations with business partners and regulators, leading to a miserable existence towards the end of their lives. Like all successful business leaders, they must have been supremely confident about themselves, believed in the infallibility of their plans and actions and given top marks to their operational styles and short-lived achievements. They almost certainly believed that their business partners, critics and regulators were either blind or lacked intelligence.

I must confess that the last few years of my corporate life, of which over two and a half years were spent with Coca-Cola India, provided a great learning and an invaluable insight into the way corporate management run their affairs and manage their reputation. While it would be foolish to generalize and paint too bleak a picture of the corporate world – undeniably, many corporate organizations, large and small are built on a bedrock of corporate ethics and a vision of consumer welfare – I was deeply disturbed by some of my personal experiences, and a few things I witnessed first hand. I once found the executive director of a closely-held company, once promoted with a UK partner, receiving his monthly pay packet (packets, to put it more correctly, as some part was in cash) from another listed company managed by the same group of promoters. In another instance, one of the country's best-managed engineering companies was seen struggling against a little-known enterprise, being part of a Rs 10 billion industrial group promoted by the son and son-in-law of a politician during his brief tenure as a minister in the Union government and reportedly funded by a Mauritius-based shell company. The engineering firm had to settle the issue through a costly buy-out deal. In yet another case, a highly qualified US returned environment engineer bodily lifted portions of an old project report of a proposed hydroelectric power plant to quickly prepare a positive environment impact assessment (EIA) report for the promoters of a power project in Karnataka. An American multinational firm, his employers, were left speechless when environmentalists leaked this out to the media. There was the case of a globally acclaimed US financial services organization which had a minority holding in a closely-held Indian firm. The US giant wanted to raise its stake in the company but was thwarted by the chairman of the original promoter, a government controlled sick financial institution, because he was jealous of the success of the offspring. The US firm got what it wanted only after that chairman retired and the financial institution itself was in bad shape. But none could match the wits of another US multinational. Upset with a somewhat evasive public statement by a state chief minister, this American multinational admonished him in writing and sent a copy of the letter to his party's national president.

In September 2001, when Coke was desperately trying to avoid its equity divestment commitment, I took up a job with Coke as Director – Corporate Affairs and Communications. I was lured by the complex nature of Coke's operations in India, the excitement the job offered and the opportunity to work as an image manager of the world's largest brand in India. I left business journalism to understand corporate organizations from within, their stresses and strains, management practices, internal intrigue, external pressures, consumer and community concerns, follies and foibles. The Coca-Cola India job offered the ideal opportunity. I quit Coke a few months after I finished my initial two-year contract by which time the company had finished with its share divestment and also its final deposition before the country's Joint Parliamentary Committee (JPC), probing into the allegation of pesticide content in Carbonated Soft Drinks (CSD) and the company's constant fight with the Perumatty Panchayat (village council) in Kerala over heavy groundwater exploitation and disposal of solid waste from its plant as manure to local farmers.

The professional management of a corporation is expected to act as a trustee of its shareholders and operate in a manner that continuously strives to raise shareholder value and stakeholder appreciation. To achieve this, the management needs to be honest and transparent in its dealings with both internal and external stakeholders and be seen as socially responsible. In practice, however, they seem to be more concerned about their narrow business objectives and personal gains. In India, it is generally propagated that business cannot be run through honest means. Many entrepreneurs say honesty has no place in business and honest managers would rather take *sanyas* (renounce worldly life) than run businesses.

Coca-Cola is an iconic brand. It is the world's largest, ahead of even the likes of Microsoft and the Big Apple. Atlanta-based The Coca-Cola Company (TCCC) has long served as a symbol of globalization and flag carrier of American capitalism. It operates out of some 197 countries across the world. The company is also probably the biggest corporate guzzler of a key natural resource, water, the base raw material for beverage making, practically free of cost in many of these countries. All these make the company's operations vulnerable to constant public gaze. At a time when more and more business and industrial corporations are being subjected to public scrutiny, the concept of corporate citizenship is no longer a fashionable buzzword. The management of large business organizations is fast changing their operational styles on the Gandhian trusteeship model. Modern B-Schools attach more importance to long-term stakeholder value than to immediate gains. Among the factors contributing to the stakeholder value are good corporate governance, high level of business transparency, management morality, business ethics and social concerns.

Unfortunately, TCCC appeared to be somewhat out of tune with the times. In India, its operations, especially between 1998–9 to 2003–4, had been constantly in the news for one wrong reason or the other because of the company's clashes with business partners and associates, government, regulators, local community and administration, non-governmental organizations (NGOs), media and the civil society overshadowing some of the small initiatives it took in the areas of rainwater harvesting and community service. Coca-Cola is not India's No. 1 brand. According to the 2007 ACNielsen ORG-MARG Survey along with *The Economic Times Intelligence Group* of 'India's most trusted brands', Coca-Cola does not feature even among the top 40. The company's locally acquired brand, Thums Up, is well ahead of Coke at 34, the highest among TCCC beverage brands in India. Rival Pepsi ranks the twentieth. The brand image of both Coke and Pepsi was badly bruised in the wake of the controversy over pesticides in colas in 2003. While Pepsi has been able to substantially recover its brand image over the next four years, the brand Coke is still languishing. The following chapters are largely about what went wrong with Coke's India operations between 1989 and 2004 and how it impacted the company's image, locally as well as globally.

Right from the day Coke's name resurfaced in the local media after it had tied up with Singapore-based Rajan Pillai to mark its re-entry into India till the company's controversy over pesticide content in its products, distribution of toxic industrial waste to farmers and depletion of groundwater in Kerala and other states, I have been witness to its troubled business journey through India, first as a media man and later as Coke's communi-cator. The Coke story is an amazing one for many reasons. It is a story of management ineptitude, arrogance and manipulation. It is a story of flagrant violation of corporate ethics. It is a story of people putting their narrow personal ambition before the company's long-term interest. It is a story of the world's largest brand being criticized by the government, the public, NGOs and global media. It is a story of a global company dumping its global management and operational principles and practices to *think local and act local* in order to grow fast in India. It is a story of poor corporate governance and lack of management morality that made large sections of the community and the company's business associates, including Indian shareholders and initial joint venture partners, feel cheated. It almost reads like fiction. I thought the subject provided all the necessary ingredients for an interesting corporate study.

In writing this book, I have tried to apply strictly an objective yardstick to chronicle, explain, interpret and extrapolate information that any professional writer would do to present his story. I have tried consciously to restrain myself from using inside documents and 'spicy' inside information and depended almost entirely on published materials, documents, the company's communication with the government, stakeholders and the media in India as well as in other parts of the world, official letters and statements, my earlier interaction as a journalist with the management of Coke, Pepsi, Parle, Britannia Industries, Groupe BSN, the Foreign Investment Promotion Board, Government of India and some of Coke's franchisee bottlers since the late

1980s. I also interacted with some of Coke's senior management team members, past and present, who have greatly helped me in understanding the internal complexities and compulsions leading to the development and management of serious incidents and crises in the company's India operations over the years. A number of these senior managers left Coke in the last few years in search of greater professional satisfaction in other well-known enterprises or in other locations in the global Coke system. Some inside knowledge of the management actions, inactions, system manipulations, self-aggrandisement are responsible for the development of various crisis situations inside the company, which are bound to be reflected in a book of this nature written by a former senior member of the company's external affairs management team. Such references are rare and restricted mostly to support or interpret information, which is otherwise in the public domain. The intention of writing this book is not to find fault with individuals but to detail the turbulent times of the world's largest manufacturer of soft drinks and a growing force in the bottled water business. The book covers the period between January 1991 and May 2004.

Coke has been at the centre of controversy for one reason or the other ever since it decided to return to India after a gap of 15 years. Even its exit in 1977 was controversial when it tried to resist a government directive to comply with the country's Foreign Exchange Regulation Act. The book chronicles the company's troubled times in the first 12 chapters. The last two chapters are more about the controversies related to its management practices in India as well as in other parts of the world.

Nantoo Banerjee
December 2008

1

Blunder at Rebirth

Rebirths are always tricky affairs; corporate rebirths are often more complicated. But one good thing about a corporate rebirth is that it isn't fortuitous: it is pretty well thought out and planned right down to the last detail. At least, that is how it should be. But Coca-Cola, the world's most valued brand, seemed to have different ideas.

In 1991, when Atlanta-based The Coca-Cola Company (TCCC), decided to return to India ending a 14-year exile, one would have expected the cola giant to have carried out an elaborate pre-investment scrutiny to validate all the reasons that justified its return to India.

In hindsight, it seems unthinkable that Coca-Cola did not bother. Or, perhaps it was just a perfunctory exercise – which probably explains why it blundered into untrustworthy relationships and less-than-transparent deals, and lurched from controversies to crises with unfailing regularity. The King of Fizz chose to return to a country at a time when it was in ferment.

The year 1990–1 was one of the most turbulent years in India's political and economic history; there was a raging political crisis within and its ruinous economy was buffeted by the aftershocks of a war in the neighbouring Gulf.

In August 1990, the late Iraqi dictator Saddam Hussein had sent his troops into Kuwait to capture the disputed Rumailah oilfields, sending a frisson of fear through the Arab world and concern in America that its considerable oil interests in the region could be severely compromised.

President George Bush Sr of the US ordered Saddam to withdraw his troops from Kuwait or face the consequences of a smackdown by global armed forces led by the US. As the shrill war of words escalated, tensions rose in the Gulf and world economies and markets shuddered as oil prices went though the roof.

The turbulence was felt in India as well, where political skulduggery had foisted two minority governments in rapid succession with temporary outside support from large national parties like the Bharatiya Janata Party (BJP) and the Congress.

Coca-Cola's return to India appeared to be badly star-crossed. Two years before, arch-rival PepsiCo had dramatically arrived on Indian shores. Coca-Cola felt it had no choice but to follow in its wake. Nevertheless, in early 1991, the situation did not look too great to plan a business venture in India. Besides the political squalls, the dark clouds of an economic crisis loomed as the country wrestled with the weight of its mounting debts. The country's foreign exchange reserves, recalls a former business editor of *The Hindustan Times* who covered the country's Finance Ministry back then, had shrunk to just US $1.2 billion on 12 January 1991, just enough to cover three weeks of the country's imports. Expatriate workers in the Gulf, who contributed a significant portion of the foreign exchange remittances into the country were returning in droves. Standard and Poor's and Moody's – the world's best-known credit rating agencies – had downgraded India's sovereign rating to junk bond status.

By early 1991, Finance Minister Yashwant Sinha was in a sweat trying to deal with a mammoth financial crisis. In an unprecedented move, he mortgaged the country's gold reserves with the Bank of England and several other central banks in Europe to raise desperately needed cash to finance imports and head off a situation where India stood in danger of defaulting on its international debt commitments. The industrial landscape really looked bleak: state-owned companies that represented the bulwark of the country's economy were awash in red; inflation had soared to double-digit levels, government spending had careened out of control and revenues were down to a trickle, rendering the exchequer parlous.

Since the start of the 1990s, several Indian economists had forecast that the country's huge borrowings from the International Monetary Fund (IMF) in the early 1980s would put a huge strain on the country, fuelling the need for a massive structural adjustment including devaluation of the Indian rupee and a stiff dose of economic reforms. Rampant *havala* (illegal transactions that funnelled black money out of the country and brought it back as legitimate dollars) further weakened the rupee and spawned a new breed of carpetbaggers – Non-resident Indians (NRIs) – who wired money through a skein of shell companies registered in tax havens like St Kitts, the Isle of Man, the Bahamas and even Mauritius.

Rajan Pillai, a small-time cashew exporter from Kerala who later set up base in Asian entrepôt Singapore, belonged to this growing band of parvenus. They had one key trait: a burning desire to make it big in the shortest possible time and did not care about the rules they bent and the corners they cut to realize their ambitions.

It was unimaginable that Coca-Cola, a Fortune 500 titan, should pick Pillai from relative obscurity as a partner in its business foray to recapture the market in India from where it had been unceremoniously booted out in 1977.

TCCC, however, was in a tearing hurry. It chose to ignore the adverse investment climate in India and the political uncertainty while planning its return to India after a gap of close to 14 years. Coke had been expelled from the country when it refused to comply with foreign investment regulations fashioned by an ill assorted band of politicians who had toppled the Indira Gandhi-led Congress Party in early 1977. And now PepsiCo, its arch-rival from New York, had already established base in India. Was that the reason why Coke chose to ignore the ground realities or why it rushed into an ill-advised joint venture with an Indian businessman with small scruples and big ambitions? Was this the only way to win back the huge Indian market it had left 14 years ago and where PepsiCo was already making waves? This time it was playing for bigger stakes: it was going to manufacture the Coke concentrate – arguably, the most closely guarded secret formula in the world. Last time around, it had merely operated as a trading company – Coca-Cola Export Corporation – importing soft drink concentrate for Indian bottlers.

Coke's poor choice of partner and the unseemly haste with which it pursued its desire to return to India would trigger the first of many controversies in which the cola giant would be embroiled in India. The events over the next 18 months would show just how horrendous those two decisions were: they would blot its carefully crafted corporate reputation and sully its brand image over the next few years.

2

Joint Venture

On 12 April 1991, Coca-Cola South Asia Holdings Inc. (CCSAH), a subsidiary of Atlanta-based TCCC, entered into a joint venture agreement with J M Rajan Pillai, a Singapore-based NRI. Did the American Multinational Corporation (MNC) investigate the NRI's credentials, his background, source of funds and determine how he 'acquired' the Britannia group of companies internationally? Or, did it gloss over such a crucial element of the due diligence process merely because the alliance helped TCCC circumvent India's tough entry conditions for multinationals in a low technology, low priority industry like fizzy drinks? The entry conditions were highly relaxed for Overseas Corporate Bodies (OCBs) with an NRI holding off at least 60 per cent. TCCC was quick to spot the advantage of taking such a route. Thus, Rajan Pillai was persuaded to establish overnight an OCB called JMRPCO Limited in Hong Kong to facilitate Coke's re-entry.

Under the terms of the shareholders agreement signed on 12 April 1991, JMRPCO Limited would promote in India a business in the field of non-alcoholic beverages, including beverage bases and essences, and processed snack foods. The agreement also envisaged the formation of another joint venture between JMRPCO and Britannia

Industries Limited christened as Britco Foods Company Pvt. Limited to handle beverage blending with its registered office in Kolkata.

JMRPCO had an authorized and issued capital of US $100,000, with each share valued at US $1. Rajan Pillai held 60 per cent of the equity capital with an aggregate value of US $60,000. The remaining 40 per cent belonged to CCSAH. It was, however, felt that the company would need US $15 million to start its business in India. The partners agreed that additional funds would be provided by TCCC in the form of 'non-interest bearing demand loans'.

The most interesting part of the agreement was the section concerning management control of the joint venture company. The company would have seven directors – three each from JMRPCO and CCSAH and one director to be jointly nominated by the two joint venture partners. The chairman's post would rotate annually between the two partners. Such an agreement is unusual as it undermines the position of the 60 per cent shareholder in terms of voting rights and management control. Did Coke use Pillai merely as a front man for the project? That was probably TCCC's original intention. But, Pillai had other ideas. It was another matter that this international corporate player would soon be exposed, almost jeopardizing Coke's entire game plan, but not before he extracted his pound of flesh from TCCC.

The agreement was a legal masterpiece. It provided for rights – in the event of changes in Indian laws – that would enable CCSAH to own and operate the beverage blending division of Britco Foods. Another clause in the agreement provided for a minimum export of not less than Rs 10 billion (approximately US $220 million) by the company's processed foods division over a period of ten years. The export obligation was an essential condition and CCSAH was entitled to terminate the venture if the obligation was not fulfilled. It was also provided that the termination of the agreement should be by way of an instrument in writing. Clause 13 provided that the agreement was subject to English law. In case of a dispute, arbitration proceedings would be held in London under the auspices of the International Chamber of Commerce. JMRPCO, in turn, entered into a shareholder agreement with Britannia Industries Limited on 1 June 1991, to set up Britco Foods in Pune in which the Hong Kong-based Coke–Pillai OCB held 66 per cent of the equity with a provision to raise it in due course to 74 per cent if permitted by domestic law. It also roped in SICOM, Maharashtra government's industrial investment corporation, which was offered 10 per cent of the equity. The remaining 24 per cent was offered to Britannia Industries. SICOM's equity participation was, however, neither here nor there. SICOM's live register of industries merely recorded Britco Foods as a financially 'assisted sector' unit in Maharashtra. Britco Foods would have two strategic business divisions – the first a 100 per cent export oriented outfit with two units, manufacturing potato chips and snack foods and the other a beverage blending unit for Coca-Cola. Each division would be under an independent Chief Executive Officer (CEO). JMRPCO and Britannia Industries also signed a non-competition agreement to clearly state that the parties would not compete anywhere in India with the business of the two divisions of Britco Foods or engage in the sale of non-alcoholic beverages or concentrates. Britannia was, however, permitted to start a bottled water business, an area where Coke had substantial worldwide interests. One reason for this could be that Coca-Cola had no initial plans to enter the Indian packaged drinking water market because it was small, punctuated by low profitability and teemed with several small-scale manufacturers.

It is important to focus on these details to understand the operational methods of large MNCs like Coca-Cola and how they compromise on good corporate governance practices when it comes to running enterprises in developing countries like India. It is another matter that American corporate high priest Coca-Cola's marriage with an Indian corporate personality like Rajan Pillai was too short-lived to have any productive use. Soon after Pillai struck the deal with Coke, he was running for cover to save himself from criminal proceedings in various parts of the world. The result: TCCC lost a lot of credibility and corporate reputation in India for courting such a partner when planning its re-entry in India.

TCCC could also have extricated itself from a sticky situation by cutting ties with Rajan Pillai as early as July–August 1991, after India's Parliamentary (Lok Sabha) elections threw up a new dispensation that provided stability in the country's political administration and embraced the World Bank–IMF tailored economic reforms package. The new Indian Prime Minister Narasimha Rao and Finance Minister Manmohan Singh, were quick to free the industry from the shackles of decades-old license-permit regime and open up the economy to Foreign Direct Investment (FDI) and external competition. The food-processing sector was among the first to benefit from these quick changes in the government policy. Inexplicably, Coca-Cola continued its engagement with Rajan Pillai until the law caught up with him. In July 1993, the government approved Coca-Cola's application to establish a wholly-owned subsidiary in India. It secured the approval automatically without resorting to other means – a clear signal that the rules of the game for doing business in India had changed forever.

In sharp contrast, the other US snack foods and beverage giant, PepsiCo, did its homework well before deciding to start business in India. Its objectives were very clear and its ways were more transparent which took full advantage of the system to enter India as a minority partner with Indian enterprises of distinction and high repute. PepsiCo came when the economy was more stable and the country's foreign exchange regulations were being liberalized despite a series of financial scandals and questionable defence purchase deals that made the last year of Rajiv Gandhi's Congress government politically rather uncomfortable.

PepsiCo did most of its groundwork in 1988. There were entry restrictions for foreign companies in non-priority industries like soft drinks. When the company entered India the following year, it roped in an Indian firm of great repute and marketing expertise, Voltas Limited, an enterprise belonging to the Tatas, India's well-known industrial conglomerate, and Punjab Agro-Industries Corporation, a state government undertaking of the country's agriculturally richest state.

The Indian government approved PepsiCo's application with a rider. The company was required to export from India products five times the value of its import of concentrates. PepsiCo accepted the condition and successfully worked with farmers in Punjab to develop high quality potatoes and tomatoes and exported chips and tomato paste among other products to meet more than its export obligation.

Entry conditions imposed by the Indian government on PepsiCo were more onerous than those imposed on Coca-

Cola. The government permitted PepsiCo to own only 44.35 per cent in its Indian arm, Pepsi Foods Limited. Its concentrate turnover was restricted to 25 per cent of its total turnover while exports had to account for 50 per cent of the company's gross annual income over a ten-year period. Even the export modality was listed: 40 per cent of the turnover from exports was required to be generated from the company's own manufactured goods and the rest 10 per cent could come from a select list of products procured from other manufacturers. Coke would have probably never accepted such conditions to restart its business in India. PepsiCo fulfilled all the conditions until the government went on an economic reform mode and allowed Coke to start its soft drinks concentrate business on a 100 per cent ownership basis in 1993. It was then that PepsiCo applied for and obtained the government's permission to increase the foreign equity to 99.97 per cent. The following year, PepsiCo decided to invest in manufacture and sale of beverages and sought approval to set up PepsiCo India Holdings Pvt. Limited with 100 per cent overseas equity holding. The new company was permitted to either directly engage in the business of beverage manufacture, marketing and distribution, or set up subsidiaries or joint ventures. Throughout this period, PepsiCo was seen as an honest and transparent company. Much of the credit for this goes to P M Sinha who steered PepsiCo's India business for over a decade.

The strategy that Sinha adopted in meeting the various statutory obligations were highly innovative as well as challenging. This helped boost PepsiCo's image and corporate reputation enormously with India's politicians, bureaucrats and the farming community. This was PepsiCo's best 'corporate social responsibility' programme without spending any money or seeking some cheap media publicity as many MNCs in India are known to be doing these days. Sinha came from a Unilever subsidiary in India called Hindustan Lever of which he was a senior board member before taking up the PepsiCo India top job. In the 1970s and 1980s, Hindustan Lever Limited (HLL) undertook export of farm products, including marine products and merchandise exports in a big way to ensure that Unilever was allowed to have majority control over the management of the Indian arm under the then existing laws guiding the operations of MNCs in low priority areas.

3

Rajan Pillai and Coke

By the end of 1992, Rajan Pillai's luck started running out as his erstwhile business partners spread over half the globe – from Paris to Wellington – raised serious questions about his functioning style. Even his 'close friends' from India, including some of the top politicians, bureaucrats, businessmen, media barons and sports personalities, who happily enjoyed Rajan's lavish hospitality in various parts of the world, from watching tennis Grand Slam matches at Roland Garros and Wimbledon to attending the Cannes Film Festival, started avoiding him as a chain of international creditors and business partners threatened criminal prosecution against him.

As a result, the future of Britco Foods became somewhat uncertain. Rajan Pillai's ability to meet his financial commitment to the project was suspect, especially after he failed to honour his commitment to business partners like F Ross Johnson and Groupe BSN in terms of purchase of shares in various companies worldwide, including Singapore and New Zealand. Pillai was in the process of losing control of Britannia Industries Limited and TCCC was extremely worried about its India project. CCSAH had already brought in US $2.19 million as its contribution towards the equity of Britco Foods. Britannia Industries had chipped in US $1.16 million. Rajan Pillai's contribution was only around US $1 million. It would require substantially larger funds to start the India business.

Pillai's claim of management control of Britannia Industries was challenged by BSN (UK) Limited in the Bombay High Court towards the end of 1992. Soon Groupe BSN of France charged Rajan with business misconduct. Pillai was summoned by the diplomatic mission of France (Commercial Affairs Department) in Singapore. Rajan, his wife Gopika Nina Pillai and several senior Pillai associates were asked to surrender their passports.

Rajan decided to play a nationalist card portraying Groupe BSN as a predator of a company that was predominantly Indian. The professional management at Kolkata-based ITC Limited (in which the BAT Company held over 30 per cent of the shares, the single largest block by any company) had successfully used a similar strategy to prevent its original British promoters from raising their stake in the company and gain management control of their former subsidiary in India. ITC's strategy worked for two reasons. First, the tobacco giant's Indian managers on the board of ITC Limited and the top brass in the Union Finance Ministry, who indirectly controlled the government-promoted Indian financial institutions, worked together to foil BAT's move. Second, the combined shareholding of these financial institutions and their voting strength was higher than BAT's. Rajan Pillai, who also maintained an excellent rapport with the powers that be in the government and institutional shareholders, could not whip up patriotic fervour following resistance from another high-profile Indian shareholder, Nusli Wadia. Pillai also did not enjoy the full support of the majority of resident Indian managers of Britannia

Industries, led by Sunil Alagh, who trusted Wadia and the company's overseas shareholders more than Pillai.

If the NRI biscuit baron – as Pillai was described by the Indian media in those days – had hoped that his conspicuous waving of the national flag would scare away the French food giant, he had a surprise coming. On 23 November 1992, Antoine Riboud, the chair of the French conglomerate, made his first public comment on BSN's ongoing tussle with Pillai. And it was not the sort of news that Pillai had hoped to hear. Riboud, who was in Hong Kong on the day, to announce the company's Asia plans at a press conference, told this author in an exclusive interview, that 'our stake in Britannia Industries Limited is not for sale'. BSN which controlled about 19 per cent of Britannia Industries through a holding company was determined to fight it out. Riboud said that BSN had major plans for India and would not allow them to be derailed by Pillai. Riboud's assertiveness suggested that Pillai's strategy to portray himself as a patriotic Indian, even though he lived in Singapore, battling a giant multinational had failed to deter the French. In the previous month, BSN had filed a suit in the Bombay High Court against Pillai and five other directors of Britannia Industries who supported him. The suit alleged that they had conspired to siphon off US $8 million through dubious cashew deals with companies that had links to Pillai. These directors and Pillai, however, denied any wrongdoing.

An anguished, if not reticent, Riboud said, 'I have never gone to any court. This is the first time'. Apart from the Bombay suit, BSN and Pillai were also embroiled in litigation in Singapore courts. That case had its origin in a US $28 million loan from Hong Kong Bank to Britannia

Brand Holdings Limited (BBHL), a Singapore-based vehicle in which Pillai and BSN both held shares. BBHL had borrowed the money two years ago to buy a former Nabisco subsidiary in New Zealand. In 1991, when the loan came up for repayment, Pillai, who was unable to generate the requisite funds, suggested that it be rescheduled over a five-year period. BSN rejected the suggestion and repaid the full amount, including Pillai's share. In other words, Pillai's debt was transferred to BSN. The French company wanted to convert this debt into equity in BBHL in an attempt to oust Pillai from the BBHL management. Riboud, however, denied the interpretation. He said BSN did not want BBHL to be saddled with so much of debt; hence the decision to repay the loans. 'The interest burden was already heavy. We did not know what would be our business tomorrow and so we decided to pay', he said. All this was hardly music to Pillai's ears. He told the Indian media that he would be able to resolve his dispute with former mentor Ross Johnson, who was also gunning for him, as he expected a big credit injection into his company from a large West Asian business group, Al Baraka. Riboud's interview and the developments involving BSN and Nabisco, on the one hand, and Pillai's, on the other, were prominently carried in *Business Standard.* Aveek Sarkar, the then editor of *Business Standard,* followed the developments in Britannia Industries very closely.

Concern over these developments compelled TCCC's north-east Europe–Africa–India group president Neville Isdell to meet Rajan Pillai in November 1992, to find out what was going on and how the next round of funding for Britco would be conducted. Rajan was believed to have assured Neville that his financial problems would be sorted out within a month or two. But Rajan's bid to obtain funds from the Arab investor, Al Baraka, fell flat in December 1992. For Coca-Cola, it was a blessing in disguise as Rajan had reportedly promised Al Baraka certain rights or interests concerning the venture with Coca-Cola. It is then that Coca-Cola decided to dump Rajan. With the government's reform process already in progress and restrictions on FDI being gradually lifted, it was possible for Coke to set up its own venture in India.

In January 1993, Coke representatives met Rajan Pillai and offered to buy him out of JMRPCO and Britannia Industries' stake in Britco Foods. Coke submitted a formal proposal to Rajan in February 1993, for its disengagement from the partnership. While the proposed disengagement proved to be as difficult and cumbersome as the engagement, CCSAH independently submitted a proposal to the Government of India on 5 April 1993, to set up a 100 per cent owned subsidiary to manufacture beverage essences and bases.

A senior executive of Coke's India Division recalled that two routes had been proposed – acquisition of 100 per cent ownership of JMRPCO or get a stand-alone approval from the Indian government to set up a wholly-owned subsidiary. Rajan was extremely angry at this. He wrote to the chairman of the Foreign Investment Promotion Board (FIPB) to reject the CCSAH application as 'inappropriate' since the latter was already associated with Britco Foods, which had a licence. The FIPB approved Coke's proposal on 2 May 1993, which made front page headlines the next day. A day later, Rajan returned to India from Atlanta, totally unaware of the development. The Indian government's Cabinet Committee on Economic Affairs (CCEA) accorded the final approval to the Coca-Cola application on 13 July 1993.

Subsequently, the government issued another letter on 10 December 1993, cancelling the original approval granted to JMRPCO Limited. By June, Coke had managed to disengage itself from Rajan Pillai and acquire Britco Foods.

Within a fortnight of the FIPB approval of Coke's application, a totally dejected Rajan Pillai was said to have demanded a compensation of US $10 million for the sale of his interest in JMRPCO and for all the efforts he had put in. Regarding Britco Foods, he said he had no authority to negotiate on behalf of either Britannia Industries or SICOM, the two other equity partners in Britco. On 15 June 1993, Rajan settled for a 'reasonable' compensation which was reportedly paid to his account at Citibank, Hong Kong.

On 10 April 1995, Rajan was held guilty of criminal breach of trust by a district court in Singapore. The court held him guilty on 22 charges of criminal breach of trust and cheating for which he faced the prospect of spending 14 years in a Singapore jail. The sentence was to be pronounced the next morning. Rajan fled Singapore the very same night to arrive in Bombay (now Mumbai). However, by then, India's Central Bureau of Investigation (CBI) was also probing into several charges of financial fraud and illegal fund transfers against Rajan Pillai. He was arrested on 4 July 1995, and lodged in Delhi's Tihar Jail. Rajan applied before the magistrate of Delhi's Tis Hazari Court handling the extradition case for permission to be shifted to a private hospital for medical examination and treatment as he suddenly developed chest pain and uneasiness. The appeal was rejected on 6 July 1995, after the CBI counsel strongly opposed it. Pillai died the next day at Deen Dayal Upadhyaya Hospital in New Delhi, while in judicial custody.

Coke's travails with Rajan Pillai did not, however, end with his death. His widow, Gopika Nina Pillai, was determined to avenge the 'defeat' of her husband at the hands of TCCC. On 18 August 2000, her lawyer Satish Maneshinde served a legal notice on Coca-Cola, seeking Rs 1 billion (approximately US $22 million) in damages. On 29 December 2000, Nina Pillai filed a criminal complaint in a Mumbai court against TCCC, Atlanta, and others including Jayadev Raja, ex-CEO of Coca-Cola India, Neville Isdell and F Ross Johnson, former Nabisco chairman. Nina's charges against the accused included cheating, criminal breach of trust, criminal intimidation, forgery, use of forged documents and criminal conspiracy. The case is still on, and the Indian public is periodically reminded of it through her media statements on the subject.

4

Business Bully

After receiving the government's approval, Coke did not waste any further time in restarting its business in the country. First, it started manufacturing soft drinks concentrate. A plant was set up at a somewhat remote hilly location near Pune, about 250 km from Mumbai. It was ready around July–August 1993. The first batch of Coca-Cola using concentrate made in India was launched in Agra, 200 km east of Delhi, in October 1993. It was produced by one of Coke's franchisee bottlers or 'bottling partner' in the company's parlance, belonging to the Ladhani family. The Ladhani brothers continue to be Coke's largest bottling partners in India.

Coke made two more smart moves in the same year. First, it bought over India's largest cola brand called Thums Up along with more than a dozen other brands belonging to Mumbai-based Parle Products. Ramesh Chauhan, India's own cola king and Parle promoter, created and nurtured some of India's best soft drink brands in history, which still reign supreme in their respective segments in the market. They include Limca (cloudy lemon) and Maaza (juice-based drink). Coke paid only US $40 million to Parle in the biggest ever local brand buy-out deal till then. In 1992–3, the Parle soft drinks brands boasted a market share of over

75 per cent. Thums Up's share of the cola market was said to be close to 80 per cent while Pepsi was struggling at below 15 per cent. Campa, the third major cola brand, owned by Coke's pre-1977 bottler Charanjit Singh of Pure Drinks, was fast vanishing from the market. The going was so good for Parle that it set up two soft drinks concentrate plants, one near Ahmedabad in Gujarat and the other at Noida in Uttar Pradesh, bordering Delhi. Both plants had to be shut down after the deal with Coke. Ironically, heads of the two Parle concentrate plants, G M Tiwari and K S Nair, later ran Coke's high-security concentrate plant and quality, research and product development facility at Pune.

Chauhan, a marketing genius and a great brand builder, is also a pioneer in India's packaged drinking water market creating a halo around his brand Bisleri, which was almost generic to mineral water in India for nearly three decades until Coke's brand Kinley temporarily overtook it in 2002. Parle not only built great local brands like Thums Up, Limca, Maaza, Gold Spot and Bisleri, but also created a huge bottler network across the country. In the 16 years since Coke was first ousted from the country by George Fernandes, the then industry minister in the short-lived Morarji Desai government, Parle's soft drinks bottling network boasted some 50-odd plants, mostly franchisee owned. Almost all these bottlers enjoyed an excellent relationship with Parle and its Chairman Ramesh Chauhan. The Coke takeover of the Parle brands left the bottlers with just two options – to either join hands with Coke or shut down operations. Coke, however, had other plans for these helpless local enterprises.

Following the buy-out, the 54 franchisee bottlers of Parle had to terminate their agreements with Ramesh Chauhan's company and enter into fresh agreements with Coke to bottle, sell and distribute the brands earlier owned by Parle. In due course, only 26 of these bottlers upgraded their facilities to launch Coke's international brands.

In the beginning, Coke tried to implement its global model for bottling business in India by promoting the concept of anchor bottlers in financial collaboration with these entities. Worldwide, Coke is principally a manufacturer and seller of soft drink concentrates. Since the company owns the brands, it is also responsible for marketing and other services for the protection of its brands. This has been highly lucrative for TCCC – high profit, low operational investment. All costs are loaded in the price of concentrates. In contrast, the bottling business is highly capital and employment intensive. The return (net margin) is very low and absolutely volume and distribution efficiency driven. Coke set up as many as four companies to push through its idea of running the Indian business through anchor bottlers. However, it neither had the patience nor the ability to sell the concept in the country. The bottlers didn't trust Coke, which was seen as a bully after it took over the Parle brands and compelled them to either work for Coke or close down. Most of these bottlers were small or medium-sized businessmen, who had investments in other businesses as well. They neither had the funds to upgrade their bottling business to match Coke's standards, nor were they inclined to merge with each other to become a formidable combine to accept Coke's challenge. While a few of them did pull down their shutters, others continued till 1998 when another new bottlers' agreement fell due.

Between 1997 and 1999, Coke's local bottling arm, HCCB, acquired the business assets of several of its licensed bottlers and started building new plants to increase the capacity. By the end of 1999, the company acquired 37 licensed bottlers out of the 54 franchisee bottlers. Today HCCB's own bottling plants account for about 70 per cent of the total beverage sale volume of the Coca-Cola system in India while only the remaining 30 per cent are handled by independently owned licensed bottlers. In certain states, the sales and distribution of beverages manufactured by HCCB is undertaken by its wholly-owned subsidiary, Hindustan Coca-Cola Marketing Pvt. Limited.

The Indian media was full of stories about Coke's alleged strong-arm tactics to make the bottlers fall in line. In fact, one of the aggrieved bottlers, who took Coke to court and lost, engaged a high-profile Public Relations (PR) professional for his campaign against Coke. These stories were routinely denied by Coca-Cola's India Division. The most critical of such stories was featured by *Businessworld*, a national business weekly with a large circulation. Coke had reportedly approached some of its bottlers and ex-bottlers to send rebuttals in the form of legal notices to the editor and publishers to ensure that they were carried at least in the 'Letters' column. Although *Businessworld* printed some of these letters, it never retracted its cover story which had considerably damaged Coke's image in India.

Coke, keen on expanding its business fast to exploit its true potential (the fizzy drinks market was growing by 10 per cent annually between 1995 and 2000), decided to acquire these bottling assets and create new ones by setting up its own plants to exercise, if possible, full control over the downstream bottling operations. A good number of bottlers saw this as an opportunity to sell their bottling assets to Coke at highly inflated prices (more on account of intangibles like 'goodwill' than the real value of the tangibles like plant, machinery, land, buildings, etc.). Coke gobbled them all up and, in the process, discovered a US $400 million hole in its otherwise deep pocket and recorded it as a business impairment loss in India in TCCC's balance sheet for 2000.

There were some ten of them who, however, refused to hand over their operations to Coke, and made the company sign bottler agreements with them. Prominent among them were the Ladhani brothers, Goenkas of Kolkata and Kandharis of Punjab. At one point of time, Coke had gone to the extent of even setting up a greenfield unit in the backyard of one of its leading bottler family in eastern India. Coke managed to coax the Marxist government in West Bengal to allot a plot of land near Kolkata, the region served by two of its bottling partners. The announcement of the project to the media was made by the then West Bengal Industrial Development Corporation (WBIDC) Chairman Somnath Chatterjee (now Lok Sabha Speaker). The bottlers, on the other hand, tapped their political influences in the state government to prevent Coke's 'evil design' from materializing. The West Bengal state government finally offered an alternate site to Coke in the industry-starved North Bengal for its proposed plant so that it would not poach on the territory of the two bottling partners.

The *Businessworld* cover story quoted a Coke bottler, Kanti Parasrampuria, as saying that 'he and his son received constant death threats and were terrorised to give in to Coke's strong-arm tactics and were forced to sell their Indore and Bhopal plants (in Madhya Pradesh) for Rs 200 million against the agreed price of Rs 410 million'.

The story went 'Coke not only plays rough, allege bottlers, but it also plays dirty'. It quoted Coke's letter of 18 September 1995, to India's FIPB chairman, seeking approval to invest US $700 million over the next ten years, saying, 'We recognise that our existing bottlers in India have played a significant role in the development of the soft drink business and they will continue to play an important role in the planned expansion of our business in the years to come. It is envisaged that the bottlers will participate in the future expansion through their involvement as potential joint venture partners in select locations. The existing bottlers will continue to benefit through such participation and partnership in our future enterprise'. And, what did Coke do? Soon after getting the permission, Coca-Cola rushed in US $600.25 million in just over three years between July 1996 and November 1999 and launched a drive to acquire more than 25 bottlers. Coke's letter said, 'The investment in the joint ventures with bottlers will be mutual and non-coercive'. *Businessworld* then quoted three of Coke's erstwhile bottlers, Ravi K Mody of Surat Beverages (Gujarat), Rajkumar Giri of Chennai Bottling (Tamil Nadu), Coke's third largest bottler in India then, and Krishan N Parikh of Jamshedpur Beverages (then Bihar) as saying that they were pushed out of business and forced to sell their plants to Coke during 1998 and 1999.

Some of the Cadbury Schweppes' Indian bottlers told *Businessworld* that they were left high and dry after the company's beverage business was taken over by the Atlanta-based Coca-Cola through an international buy-out deal in December 1998. Schweppes operated in 155 countries. In India, it had 19 bottlers. A joint statement issued on 21 December 1998, by the representatives of the two companies in India said that it was the intention of TCCC to honour all existing agreements with Cadbury Schweppes Beverages India Limited's business partners in the country. Most of these bottlers had little choice but to shut down their operations within the next three years as Coke made little effort to make good on its 'intention'.

Having failed to implement its time tested business model of operating through anchor bottlers in India, Coke decided to wind up or merge those shell companies registered earlier for the purpose. An amalgamation arrangement scheme was drawn up in 1997–8, after Coca-Cola received a conditional licence on 17 July 1997, through its wholly-owned overseas subsidiary, Hindustan Coca-Cola Beverages Holdings Pvt. Limited (HCCH), to set up and operate a downstream bottling company in India under the name of Hindustan Coca-Cola Beverages Pvt. Limited (HCCB). The rider was that HCCH would divest 49 per cent of its equity in HCCB in favour of the Indian shareholders within five years or by 16 July 2002. The reason behind this mandatory divestment requirement, according to Donald Short, former president of Coca-Cola's India Division was that the company must give back a part of its holding to Indians from whom it acquired the bottling asset. Donald Short told me over lunch at Delhi's Taj Mahal Hotel on Man Singh Road in 1997 that they would fulfil their divestment obligations well within the due date. Coca-Cola (HCCH) failed to do it and became a target of ridicule in the media, the government, the investor community and among some of its bottling partners.

5

Legal Cobweb

The scheme of arrangement for amalgamation (actually winding up) of five subsidiaries meant to operate as anchor bottlers in four regions of India was drawn up in two parts. The companies involved were: Britco Foods, Hindustan Coca-Cola Bottling South West Pvt. Limited (HCCSW), Hindustan Coca-Cola Bottling Northwest Pvt. Limited (HCCNW), Bharat Coca-Cola Bottling Northeast Pvt. Limited (BCCNE) and Bharat Coca-Cola Bottling Southeast Pvt. Limited (BCCSE). Barring Britco Foods, the other four subsidiaries had a common address for their registered office.

The scheme as explained in legal language is quite interesting and explains the operational complexity of the parent TCCC in various parts of the world, taking legal shelter under a host of interconnected subsidiaries and corporate entities probably keeping in mind future 'eventualities'.

All the four transferor companies had a combined subscribed and paid up capital of only Rs 4,020, equivalent to US $100 at the existing exchange rate in 1998. The cost of registering these companies and their merger, including legal expenses, must have been several times more than the combined subscribed capital of these useless enterprises.

The real reason for opening and shutting down these corporate entities was never explained. Maybe, it was not required under India's Companies Act, 1956, a baggage from the British Raj. Under the law, such schemes of amalgamations are required to be advertised in newspapers in the 'Public Notices' column and they automatically become public knowledge and subject to speculation.

Coca-Cola believes in operating in circles within circles in countries outside the US. Possibly most MNCs follow such legal incorporation practices that, on hindsight, would appear more beneficial to law firms than the shareholders of these transnational corporations. If the parent companies were required under listing rules to attach profit and loss accounts of all their subsidiaries and subsidiaries' subsidiaries across the world with their main balance sheets and annual reports for business transparency, they would probably spend more time in preparing balance sheets than doing the real business.

The chart of Coca Cola's corporate structure (provided at the end of the book) is an example of how complex the parenthood or ownership of Coke's India operations could be. The interconnections relate to Coke's India operations till 2002. One of the most interesting insights provided by this chart is the incorporation of a company registered under the name of Hindustan Coca-Cola Marketing Company Pvt. Limited, as a subsidiary of HCCB, with a paid up equity capital of only Rs 20 which is less than 50 cents. Until recently no one in Coke's India Division wanted to talk about this company and the real purpose behind its incorporation.

6

Shares Disinvestment

Coke was allowed to set up an initial 100 per cent bottling subsidiary under the condition that the holding company (HCCH) would disinvest 49 per cent stake in its operating arm, HCCB, in favour of Indian shareholders within five years. HCCB received approval on 17 July 1997. Thus, it was mandatory that Coke should complete its divestment process by 16 July 2002. Coke accepted the condition although some said Coke volunteered to divest in favour of the Indians at the time of seeking licence for downstream operations in the wake of public criticism that after taking over India's best soft drinks brands, it was out to gobble up the 'poor' Indian bottlers. Coke already had another 100 per cent subsidiary, Coca-Cola India Pvt. Limited (name changed from Britco Foods), manufacturing concentrates or beverage essence and bases for its licensed bottlers.

It was clear as early as 2000 that Coke was not keen to stick to its disinvestment commitment. The reasons were mainly two. First, Coke had by then burnt its fingers through reckless purchase of some of the Indian-owned bottling companies at exorbitant prices (largely on account of goodwill as it was clarified in its balance sheet). At the end of 2000, HCCB showed an inflow of Rs 33.08

billion (over US $785 million) towards its equity. The value of this investment eroded substantially as Coke made huge losses in its bottling operations between 1997 and 2000. It implied that a capital issue would mean a distress sale of Coca-Cola shares in India – a proposition which was unacceptable to the high priests in Atlanta as it would have badly bruised the company's brand image and reputation globally. The second reason was that as the process of economic reform was evolving, it was no longer mandatory for a foreign entrant in the food processing business in 2001 to have Indian shareholding at all. By early 2002, the government even allowed Indian stock exchange listed foreign companies to buy-back Indian shares from the market. In fact, a good number of MNCs in India took this opportunity to buy-back their stocks from local shareholders.

Around the third quarter of 2001, Coca-Cola formally approached the FIPB of India with an application listing the details of its huge investment in bottling operations and its miserable performance. The application sought the waiver of the divestment clause or that the company be allowed to retain its present holding and corporate status for a period of another five years by when it would be ready for the necessary divestment. In short, it wanted a further extension of the deadline for divestment if not the deletion of the divestment clause itself.

Within days, copies of Coke's application were doing the rounds in the media, thanks to some of the company's external advisors turned adversaries. The multi-edition financial daily, *Business Standard* ran the story as a page one flier on 2 October 2001, under the headline 'Coke seeks IPO waiver as losses mount to Rs 21.78 billion' (as on 31 March 2001) and said that the cola giant planned to wipe out the losses by 2005–6 'without taking into consideration the impairment loss of Rs 14 billion'. The Coke application signed by Gabriel J Pataky, then HCCH director, said 66 per cent of the total investment had been lost and the book value of the share of Rs 10 each had declined to Rs 3. The company made a net loss of Rs 184 million during 2000–1 and was expected to break even in 2001–2.

Coke's application seeking divestment waiver or an extension of the divestment time limit said the company had given other arguments for dropping the divestment clause. One, the divestment clause had not been emphasized by the government in the last two years while clearing FDI proposals unless specifically asked for by the concerned ministry. In fact, the government has also done away with the divestment clause in several sectors. Two, the company was unable to meet the three-year profitability criteria laid down by the Securities and Exchange Board of India (SEBI) for a company planning Initial Public Offer (IPO). And, finally, no other country in the world has imposed such a condition on the company. Coke changed its tone substantially in later correspondence with the government, saying the question of IPO never arose as the requirement was nowhere specifically mentioned in the original approval letter.

It further stated: 'The plea comes within 10 months of the company urging the government to allow it more time to come out with a public issue, and the subsequent denial by the regulators on the grounds that it was too early to consider the case since the divestment clause has to be met only by mid-2002. At that time the government had made no mention of a possible deletion of the clause despite the disinvestment clause having been done away with as a policy matter in several sectors. However, it had asked the company to re-apply in the second half of 2001'.

For the next 17 months, Coke's move to duck its divestment obligations received wide media attention all over the world. Bloomberg, Reuters and Agence France Presse picked up a good part of these stories. The company's corporate reputation was totally damaged. The then Union Industry Minister Murasoli Maran, who represented a regional party called Dravida Munnetra Kazhagam (DMK) from Tamil Nadu in Prime Minister Atal Behari Vajpayee's multi-party National Democratic Alliance government, was most hostile towards Coke as the company tried to bring him under political pressure through the prime minister's office. Maran was adamant and told the beat reporters in Delhi's Udyog Bhavan that Coke had to keep its entry-level commitment.

Coke did try its best to circumvent Maran and his stance on divestment. It even tried to get the US to intervene and put political and diplomatic pressure on the Indian government on the divestment issue. US Ambassador Robert Blackwill had taken up the matter with the prime minister's Principal Secretary Brajesh Misra. A former minister and a Parliament member from the opposition Congress Party, Margaret Alva, wrote a personal letter to the Law, Justice and Company Affairs Minister, Arun Jaitley, to take a more lenient view on Coke's divestment. The letter was promptly leaked out to the media. Although Coke did not appear to be embarrassed, the otherwise high-profile Congress parliamentarian was. Incidentally, Coke's legal department was headed at that time by Joel Peres, Margaret Alva's nephew. All this made up delightful stories for the media. The bottom line was: expose Coke's manipulative practices. Bureaucrats in both the vital Industry and Economic Affairs ministries turned against the company. Even some of the senior members of BJP took strong exception to Coke's ways. A large number of politicians, bureaucrats, media persons and opinion leaders turned against the company on the divestment issue.

Meanwhile, Coke came under fire from India's investor community and stock market circles after it was clear that the company, if forced to divest, would do so only through private placement of shares with a limited few. Coke maintained that the approval letter from the government clearly required it to divest 49 per cent of its shares in the bottling company in favour of Indian shareholders. Coke was, therefore, free to make a private placement of shares with a few chosen resident Indian investors and would, certainly, not go for an IPO and stock cxchange listing. This led to a big debate in the media on Coke's corporate morality, taking shelter behind the letter and not the spirit of the law under which the company was required to divest its shares. The critics said through private placement Coke wanted to operate as a 'closely held' company keeping its business activity a secret and away from public gaze. Leading the media debate was one of the country's leading stock market analysts, Prithvi Haldea of Prime Data Base. Coke, trying desperately to delay the divestment deadline, paid little attention to public criticism. The company's books were in such a pathetic state that it would require another write-off or a massive financial and capital restructuring before it could lure even a single Indian investor to buy its shares. It pleaded for at least a two-year extension of the divestment deadline although mentally it was prepared to accept even a one-year reprieve. But, Maran kept the company guessing until the penultimate date of completing the divestment commitment under the government's original letter of approval. The high tension drama reached its climax during the first fortnight of July 2002, as nobody knew what Maran's men planned to do. The company was heading towards a 1977-like situation when it was forced to shut down its operation for failing to comply with the overseas equity dilution requirement under the Foreign Exchange Regulation Act, 1973.

Coke had a contingency plan for 'the worst case scenario' under preparation with the help of some merchant bankers, issue managers and legal advisors. But, the problem was to find willing investors. The size of the issue was also a matter of concern. Given the company's financial health, few were willing to invest in a pure equity instrument. Banks, financial institutions and public trusts demanded a guaranteed return on their investment. Many did not see much of a future in HCCB shares. In the past, too, Coke had faltered on its business projections in India.

Finally, a day before the expiry of the revised divestment deadline, 16 August 2002, the government announced the extension of the deadline by just a month. This provided Coke some breathing space although there was no way that it could complete the divestment within a month. The company, however, responded smartly by submitting within the revised date its divestment blueprint to the government, which involved financial restructuring and a routine permission from the Delhi High Court, and pleaded for further six months to complete the entire divestment process. The government agreed after it received the divestment road map and a fresh commitment from the company. On 28 August 2002, the government asked HCCH to complete Indian participation of more than 10 per cent in downstream HCCB by 17 October 2002, and the balance amount (nearly 39 per cent), by 28 February 2003. HCCB managed to list the names of four Indian shareholders as of 17 October 2002 with Class A shares. This included HCCB's two employee trusts with a combined holding of 40,500,120 shares of Rs 10 each. The two other shareholders were J B Dadachanji and Ravinder Narain, each with a ridiculously low number of four shares of Rs 10 each. So much for compliance with the government order!

Coke issued a press release on the last day, 16 August 2002, announcing its divestment road map. It said HCCH, the holding company, was offering 49 per cent of its equity in HCCB, the bottling subsidiary, to resident Indian shareholders at the face value of Rs 10 per share. Of this, 39 per cent would be allotted to private investors and business partners. The balance 10 per cent would be divested in favour of two HCCB employees' welfare and stock option trusts on the basis of 5 per cent each. HCCH hoped to complete the divestment process in as short a span of time as practically possible. The press release mentioned that the company had retained the services of ICICI Securities (merchant banker) and ABN AMRO Corporate Finance to advise on the divestment and identify potential investors. The law firm of Amarchand & Mangaldas was the legal advisor.

The news also carried a brief background of the company which said that HCCB owned and operated 26 plants and 60 distribution centres located across India. In addition, it had 20 contract packers to augment its production capacity and to cater to the increasing demand for its wide portfolio of beverages. The Coca-Cola system in India directly employed over 7,000 workers. For every direct job in the system, seven indirect jobs were created in the supply chain. Alex von Behr, President, Coca-Cola India said: 'We are happy to bring in significant Indian ownership and broad-base the stakeholders in our beverage business like we have done elsewhere around the world. We are also delighted to include employees as beneficiaries of this action. We continue to see a bright future for our company in India'. HCCB said it was in the process of becoming a complete beverage company. The promise of Indian ownership, however, proved otherwise as Indian shareholders were later denied voting rights.

Throughout its equity divestment programme, Coke kept changing its position with regard to the various implementation modalities and presented new suggestions and pleas for fresh concessions from the government. Maybe, the idea was to constantly confuse the government to such an extent that it would end up allowing the company whatever additional concessions it wanted to complete the divestment. Coke's ways became embarrassing for the government since each move of the company was being leaked out to the media thanks to certain bureaucrats and senior officials who were extremely angry with the company's ever changing position on the divestment issue. The tone and tenure of some of the company's correspondence with the government offended these officials. Coke often sounded the threat of pulling out investment from the country. Both the company and the government knew fairly well about the impracticability of such threats. The letters were badly drafted, their addresses incomplete, their language impolite and full of careless mistakes.

Coke's divestment related applications to the government undermined the basic knowledge and intellectual capability of Indian bureaucrats dealing with industrial investment and company affairs. The argument put forward for conversion of a part of its investment into preference shares was not correct, which Coke was fully aware of. It was only meant to confuse the government. Probably, Coke thought the Indian bureaucrats in the departments of Industry and Economic Affairs were incapable of reading between the lines. To attract outside equity investors, Coke had no choice but to resort to financial re-engineering of the messy capital structure of its Indian bottling arm, HCCB, mainly for two reasons. They were: huge capital base (investment was more than sales turnover) and huge accumulated losses. The exercise was intended to keep the equity portion low to make the size of its fresh equity offer to Indian investors reasonably small and manageable. Another objective was to ensure a more respectable equity to turnover ratio in the balance sheet to raise the comfort level of these investors. What happens to the 'surplus' amount in the books after downsizing the issued and subscribed equity capital? It could be shown either as an interest-free long-term loan or preference shares with 'zero' coupon rate since no government would agree on conversion of FDI into interest bearing debt. FDI means equity inflow and not debt. It was also arrogant and unbecoming of a global enterprise like Coke to interpret that the written down losses of Rs 20.86 billion (US $423 million) in the balance sheet may be regarded as 'a foreign equity investment on a non-repatriable basis'. Did it imply that India should remain beholden to Coke for its business inefficiency as it indirectly benefited the country and its central bank's dollar reserves? The argument was certainly not in good taste. Coke was equally wrong to suggest that it had an option to repatriate the amount (Rs 8.03 billion) lying 'unutilised in the advance against share capital account' in the process of capital restructuring. This was fictional. The fact was that every cent of Coke's FDI in India was utilized. The surplus existed only on paper, emerging out of the redistribution or redefinition of capital under various heads, after taking care of the losses and keeping the equity capital low. Therefore, there was no way Coke could repatriate this capital if the government rejected its plea for conversion of the equity into interest bearing loan or preference shares. The money was all invested in business. Nothing was available for repatriation unless Coke sold its business. In the end, it was a meaningless threat, which Coke did not pursue.

Coke's final divestment timetable became big news all over the country and other parts of the world and brought relief to the beleaguered company. But, it proved to be short-lived as the company's next application to the government, seeking permission to issue non-voting shares to Indians, was all over the media again.

The plea was promptly turned down by the Union Finance Ministry (Economic Affairs Department). A fresh debate on Coke's divestment started. Ultimately, a note from the Department of Company Affairs, which endorsed the existence of such a provision, did the trick. Moreover, there were no complaints from Coke's new Indian shareholders and the company continued to be a private limited one after the divestment. Around September 2002, the government approved Coke's prayer. It came as a consolation and great relief although many felt that Coke cheated Indian shareholders. The HCCB board of directors did not have even a single private Indian shareholder representative on it. It comprised only four members – Sanjiv Gupta, then deputy president of India Division, Michel Blanchard, general manager of Varoise de Concentres SA, a Coke holding company in France, N Shridhar and Rajiv Sarin, both local senior executives. The sale of shares did not carry any management rights or position on the board of directors.

Coke's petition before the Delhi High Court on 10 September 2002 provides some interesting insights into its financial window dressing before engaging itself in private placement of HCCH shares in HCCB. The petition was submitted before Justice Vikramjit Sen through Arun Jaitley, senior advocate, with S S Shroff as advocate. The former law minister was briefly out of the government then. The company also pleaded that local newspapers or reporters may not be allowed to see the judgement, nor should it be reported in the *Law Digest.* The petitioner, HCCB, said it proposed to carry out a reduction of the amount standing in its Security Premium Accounts 'from Rs 21,000,000,000 to Rs 138,561,307'.

The reason given was that the company proposed to 'adjust its business impairment losses of Rs 14,000,000,000 and accumulated losses of Rs 6,761,850,805 aggregating to Rs 20,761,850,805 as on 31 March 2001 against the amount preserved in its Security Premium Accounts. It is stated that through this exercise the company will reflect its capital value as its assets value base diminution, rather than actual losses brought forward'. It was stated that the company did not have secured creditors and in any case, the rights and interests of the creditors would not be affected since the company would have sufficient net worth after adjustments.

HCCB's current assets as on 26 July 2002 were over Rs 12.52 billion whereas its current liabilities and provisions were Rs 9.64 billion. The net current asset after taking into account the current liabilities and provisions stood at Rs 2.88 billion. 'Assuming the confirmation of the reduction of the Security Premium Account, there shall be no change in the issued and paid up capital and the Security Premium Account shall be to the extent of Rs 13,85,61,307', the petition said. The matter was advertised in the Delhi edition of *Hindustan Times* and Mumbai edition of *The Times of India* to inform the public that it would be up for hearing on 2 December 2002.

The capital structure of HCCB as on 16 August 2002, showed the company's authorized share capital at Rs 6 billion from 600 million shares carrying a face value of Rs 10 each. There were three types of shares – Class A equity (350 million), Class B equity (150 million) and Preference (100 million). The issued, subscribed and paid up capital was a little over Rs 4.05 billion, including the value of 105 million equity shares held by the holding company HCCH. In addition, there was a component of Rs 8.0336 billion as advance against share capital received from HCCH. The 105 million Class B shares were issued to HCCH at a premium of Rs 200 per share, creating a share premium account of Rs 21 billion. The ultimate financial jugglery showed no free reserves or surplus.

Contrary to the media hype created by the Coke's management in India about the size of the carbonated soft drinks (CSD) business (Rs 70 billion) and its market share (60 per cent), HCCB's audited balance sheet, which is not a public document, for the year ended 31 March 2001, showed the company's gross turnover at only Rs 14.71 billion against a total expenditure of Rs 15.54 billion.

And, the company incurred a loss of over Rs 826 million. HCCB, according to Coke's own admission, accounts for nearly 70 per cent of Coca-Cola's beverage business in India. Coke's franchisee bottlers account for the rest.

The question is, why did Indian investors pick up HCCB's junk equity shares at par value of Rs 10 or for that matter at any value since its profit prospects were always suspect. Who were these investors? Coke said, in a press statement that the company's present and ex-bottlers were among the investors. What was the subscribed amount from this bottling community? If the bottling community's contribution was extremely low, could it be because it had little faith in HCCB's management? Or, was it because it did not want shares without voting rights? Coke's franchisee bottlers and contract bottlers are not known to be running their operations at a loss, but HCCB does. Indian stakeholders deserve answers to these simple questions from a global enterprise, which often talks about its good corporate governance practices and transparency. Although Coke's bottling arm has been incurring losses, its 100 per cent owned concentrate manufacturing company, Coca-Cola India Pvt. Limited, having a single factory in Pune, Maharashtra, has been earning huge profits.

The financial market gossip was that Coke's private placement was more like a debt than an equity instrument with the investors, mostly institutional trusts. It promised an attractive return on investment irrespective of the company's profit and loss. There was also a share buy-back provision. The company denied these 'rumours'. The comprehensive transaction term sheet prepared by ICICI Securities, the merchant banker cum financial advisor, which did an excellent job for Coke in detailing the divestment road map, provided for three very crucial arrangements for protecting Indian investments in HCCB shares. They were: escrow arrangement, capital gains sharing arrangement and safety net arrangement. 'Within 30 days of receipt of notice of a trigger point from HCCH, the purchasers shall have the right to, by written notice, notify HCCH of their intention to exercise the safety net, failing which the right to exercise the safety net on account of the trigger event, shall be deemed to have lapsed. The rights and obligations of each of the parties in respect of the safety net will be recorded in a safety net agreement.'

Under the arrangement, the holding company, HCCH, was required to appoint an escrow agent on or before the transaction date. The escrow agent would pay the safety net price to the purchasers. The obligation for payment of the safety net price by the escrow agent would be fully secured by an acceptable bank. The capital gains sharing agreement would become effective if at the end of a 36-month period, the purchaser decided to retain the sale shares. It was also stated that the earn out capital would be equal to a 20 per cent yield per annum on the purchase price (therein reducing the dividends, if any, paid by HCCB on sale shares from the transaction date till the date of sale).

HCCH would provide an option to the purchasers to sell and transfer their portion of the sale shares (in whole and not in part) to an acquirer identified by HCCH, eligible to acquire the sale shares as per the prevailing laws, on the safety net date at the safety net price. If the safety net date occurred on or prior to 12 months from the transaction date, then the safety net price would be Rs 11.10. If the date occurred after 12 months and on or prior to 24 months from the transaction date then it would be priced at Rs 12.32 and, if it occurred after 24 months and on or prior to 36 months then it would be priced at Rs 13.68. In all such cases, the price payable implies fewer dividends on the sale shares paid by HCCB, from the transaction date to the safety net date. The two HCCB employee trusts, having a combined holding of a little over 10 per cent, have not been provided with any special or contractual exit rights or an option to sell and transfer their shares to HCCH or any acquirer identified by HCCH, on the safety net date and safety net price.

For a simple equity issue, such exit conditions and safety net provisions are unheard of. Time alone will tell how the relationship between Coke and its 39 per cent Indian non-voting shareholders develops in the coming years. Indian investors had expected Coke to be honest and transparent in meeting its divestment commitment. The actual divestment, however, turned out to be mere eyewash. Few will trust Coke after this.

7

The Poor Third

Since its first relaunch in Agra in October 1993, Coke has spent millions of dollars in advertising and marketing its brand in India to occupy consumer mind space, boost brand preference and increase its market share. In the process, the company took some thoughtless decisions, which not only thwarted the growth of its total business, but also led to a loss of opportunity to make the life of its international rival, PepsiCo, more difficult in the Indian market.

After acquiring India's largest Cola brand, Thums Up, along with other top local soft drinks brands from the Parle stable, the company decided to 'kill' Thums Up to promote brand Coca-Cola. While the latter had the lion's share of Coke's advertisement and marketing expenditure over the years, it nearly stopped spending on the brand Thums Up, which accounted for nearly 80 per cent share of the Cola market until 1993. PepsiCo, which was not allowed to use its international brand name initially as an entry condition, really struggled for a toehold in the local market against massive consumer preference for Thums Up.

Coke, instead of cashing in on the huge popularity of Thums Up, tried to destroy the brand by sharply slashing its advertisement and marketing expenditure and cutting shelf space and availability of the 'rival' in-house cola brand in retail outlets to build and boost its international brand in India. However, consumers rejected the move. An increasing number of Thums Up 'addicts' took to Pepsi in several markets where Thums Up marketing, sales and distribution were deliberately choked to promote Coca-Cola. In the process, Pepsi made a big progress over both Thums Up and Coca-Cola. Coke's lopsided and self-injurious marketing policy during 1993–9 came under flak in the Indian media and became a subject of 'case study' for students of marketing in B-Schools as well as for marketing professionals, young and old, in India. During this period, the company became so insensitive to the intellect of the Indian consumers that it was 'dumping' its cheap American Coke commercials having little relevance or consumer-connect on the Indian society and ethos. This turned many consumers against the brand.

It took almost seven years after the company's relaunch and its inability to 'kill' Thums Up and replace the latter's market share with Coca-Cola for the management to accept that its marketing and distribution policies with regard to the acquired Indian cola brand was a 'blunder'. So strong is the brand Thums Up that despite years of neglect and stepfatherly treatment by its owners, the Thums Up juggernaut rolled on in terms of sales volume and market leadership. Since 2000, Coke has increased its advertisement budget on Thums Up and curtailed its unrealistic brand promotion programme. The marketing communications have also undergone a sea change over the last few years. The focus has shifted to Indian consumers, both urban and rural, taking into account their lifestyles, likes and dislikes, preferences and prejudices. In 2003, Coca-Cola commercials received some of the best advertisement industry awards in the country. However, it is another matter that these awards and accolades for creative excellence and the use of some of the country's most popular and expensive film stars as brand ambassadors did not get translated into brand Coca-Cola's market share in India.

The brand Coca-Cola's share of the company's marketing and advertisement expense continues to be disproportionate to its sales volume, market share and profit earning potential compared to its other in-house cola brand, Thums Up. The latter continues to be the right choice for cola drinkers in most parts of the country and especially in Andhra Pradesh, Maharashtra and West Bengal, where Thums Up's market share varied from 60 per cent to almost 80 per cent. Incidentally, all the three top Parle brands – Thums Up, Limca and Maaza were still the best-selling brands in their respective categories in the market segment. In terms of revenue, their combined contribution to HCCB's annual operational income was simply overwhelming compared to international brands like Coca-Cola, Fanta and Sprite. Unfortunately, Coke is often uncomfortable and apologetic about the continuing success of the Indian brands led by Thums Up.

Coke is among the country's biggest advertisement spenders. Its advertisement and marketing budget is variously estimated at Rs 1.2–1.8 billion annually. The company's stock response to the media on advertisement expenditure is that it represents only around 5 per cent of the India Division's turnover. The Division comprises both the HCCB-owned operations and franchisee operations. And, the company's media statements on Coca-Cola India's turnover in the past varied according to the moods of its top management until the bosses from Hong Kong and Atlanta warned the Indian managers against sharing numbers (top line, bottom line and monthly or quarterly business growth and so on) with the Indian public towards the end of 2002. The business is private. Under Indian law, the company or the division is not required to make public announcements of its performance – physical or financial. Assuming that the division's turnover would be around Rs 40 billion, the advertisement and marketing budget would be around Rs 2 billion. Whatever be the advertisement expense, nearly 60 per cent or more was on account of the brand Coke. That is a huge amount by Indian standards for any single brand.

In spite of the ever increasing advertisement cost, affordability drive through price cut, availability push through rural market penetration and strong on-the-ground programme to boost sales, brand Coca-Cola's market share seems to be declining. It remained the 'third cola' in India's CSD market, which grew by over 100 per cent during the ten-year period (1994–2003). At the end of 2003, Thums Up continued to lead the pack with a market share of close to 23 per cent with Pepsi running almost neck and neck with over 21 per cent and the pampered Coca-Cola moving into the distant third position with a market share of around 11 per cent. In fact, Coke's market share had dipped during 2003. The company's falling public image and its constant entanglement in public controversies seems to have adversely affected the consumer preference for the brand Coca-Cola. Coke's Indian brands still rule supreme. But for their presence by now, Coke would probably have had second thoughts about its India operations.

Coke's experiment with brands in India has been less than rewarding with the exception of the retail packaged drinking water, Kinley. Since 2000, Coke had launched a number of new products, flavours and brands. It also inherited some of the most talked about Schweppes brands in India. While the latter are almost non-existent in the market, the company's experiment with the energy drink 'Shock' was a disaster. Shock was launched with fanfare and promoted as a lifestyle product in select markets through hand-picked outlets to project it as a niche drink. The punch line used was 'unleash the beast in you' (whatever that may have meant). The presence of Korean Ginseng and Brazilian Guarna as ingredients in the drink was supposed to do the job. It was initially priced at Rs 30 a bottle, making it the most expensive locally manufactured non-alcoholic beverage. Imported energy drink brands were three times more expensive. The size of the Indian market for such drinks was said to be close to Rs 1 billion. And, the profit margin was claimed to be very attractive. The campaign lasted for nearly five months. It got huge media coverage and good response from consumers. But, for reasons best known to the company and least known to the consumers, Shock disappeared from the market within a year in 2002. The company's marketing head told the media that the product was being relaunched while the corporate office denied any such move.

If Shock was the highest priced Coke brand to fail in the Indian market within months of its high pitched launch, Sunfill, a powdered drink, priced at only Rs 2 per single serve sachet, launched in 2002, was fast disappearing from the market since the middle of 2003. The Sunfill TV commercial was highly appealing. A multiple-channel distribution system was engaged to make sure Sunfill sachets were available even in the smallest of small grocery outlets in small towns across the country. In some markets, the stocks were being cleared on a 'buy one, get one free' basis. Yet, the product created a huge problem in the Tamil Nadu market because of its quality deterioration, leading to product recall in some cases. This was done quietly. Like Shock, Sunfill too was a great idea. The size of the powdered drink market in India is estimated at close to Rs 1.50 billion. It had tremendous growth potential because of the low price but Coke's sudden indifference towards Sunfill is as inexplicable as its decision to dump 'Shock'. Coke used contract packers to manufacture Sunfill. Some of these small-scale manufacturers were the worst hit by the company's decision.

Similarly, its much hyped 'test' launch of Georgia tea and coffee, priced as low as Rs 4 to Rs 5 per cup in 2002 failed to tap the potential of the vast out-of-home, ready-to-drink hot tea/coffee market. According to market sources, Coke was able to place only some 4,000 machines in certain select areas to pursue the business, pioneered in India by Hindustan Lever and Nestle, which is an international beverage partner of Coke in tea and coffee. Suddenly, Coke became tight-lipped about its tea and coffee plans. Coke's own study of the market size of various non-alcoholic beverages in India in 2001 estimated the size of soft drinks market at 1.76 billion litres, retail packaged drinking water at 1.05 billion litres, tea at 21.26 billion litres, coffee at 1.12 billion litres and milk at 26 billion litres. The company said its entry into the lucrative ready-to-drink hot tea and coffee market is part of its corporate objective to lead a 'beverage revolution' in

India. The company's top bosses expressed, from time to time, Coke's plans to diversify into packaged tender coconut water, milk and milk-based products, *nimbu-pani* (fresh lime water), 100 per cent juices, etc. Market sources, however, say that Coke is not going to take any chances after it modified its business strategy to selling CSD at Rs 5 for 200 ml and Rs 6 for 300 ml in 2003. The prices have since been raised. Low-priced Sunfill and Georgia tea and coffee could challenge the success of the five-rupee soft drinks.

For TCCC, the CSD business has proved to be the best and most profitable for over 115 years. It operates in some 197 countries following almost a uniform business strategy and tactics. The only exception is Japan, where its ready-to-drink coffee business under the Georgia brand is probably bigger than its fizzy drinks business. Back home, its CSD business is facing increasing resistance from NGOs and public health lobbyists. The CSD business in North America is stagnating, forcing the company to diversify into non-alcoholic health and energy drinks and packaged drinking water, which has several competing local and global brands. The diversified business is more challenging and less profitable. The CSD business is easy money. This explains why Coke's highly diversified North American business, which accounts for about 30 per cent of its global volume and nearly 40 per cent of its global operating revenue, generates only around 24 per cent operating profits. Compared to this, nouveau riche Asia, which accounts for only around 17 per cent volume, contributes almost 25 per cent to the global operating revenue and nearly 30 per cent to the total operating profit. Japan, the Philippines and China account for over 60 per cent of the Asian business volume. China and

India, where business is relatively new, are the two large emerging markets with huge business potential. The Indian business is growing at the rate of 10 per cent annually. The business was somewhat flat in 2001. The following year, however, the Indian volume grew by around 30 per cent, the highest in the Asia-Pacific region. Recent controversies over pesticides residue content in fizzy drinks stifled Coke's growth in India during the later part of 2003.

In India, Coke is mainly into its basic business of manufacturing and selling CSD products. It is a simple concoction. The popular in-house description of the products and technology in the Coke family around the world is, 'it does not involve any rocket science'. All it involves is the preparation of syrup in two stages – raw syrup and ready syrup. Raw syrup involves mixing of sugar with hot water and the process of purification of sugar syrup. The raw syrup is mixed with specified concentrate (an aromatic concoction made of raw fruit juice and other agents, including malic, citric or phosphoric acid) in accordance with mixing instructions or TCCC's proprietary formulae. The water used to manufacture soft drinks is treated to remove oxygen to avoid reactions which destroy aromatic substances. A multi-barrier process is used for the treatment of water depending upon its source (borewell or municipal supply) either through reverse osmosis or softening followed by lime coagulation. In case of CSD, the water is 'carbonated' with carbon dioxide under high pressure.

The success of the CSD business can be attributed to the marketing and advertising drive rather than the intrinsic value of these products. Although the high pitch marketing and advertising lures millions of youths, the brands themselves are under constant attack from educational institutions, public policymakers and social activists in the US and Europe. There is a growing campaign against junk food and soft drinks and their ill effects on the human body, especially on growing children, who are the biggest consumers of such food and drinks. The adverse effects include obesity, osteoporosis, diabetes and cancer. This has forced TCCC to go on the defensive in these countries explaining the effects of aspartame, caffeine, sugar, etc. The key message is – CSD products are safe and so are the ingredients where aspartame is not a health risk. Caffeine has no negative impact on hydration or bone health. There is no connection between cardiovascular disease, cancer and caffeine; sugar consumption has not been shown to cause obesity and soft drinks are not a major contributor to tooth decay. However, not all members of the scientific community agree with Coke and to its reference to select scientific study reports.

In India, lately a new dimension has been added to the question of utility of these CSD, following the report of a Joint Parliamentary Committee (JPC) that pulled up both Coke and Pepsi on pesticide residues in their products. The interesting part of the anti-Cola campaign is that modern consumers are not only looking for merely 'safe' products, but also for products that are healthy. Coke has been assertive in its defence for whatever it does and for whatever it is worth. And, this is making the brand increasingly unpopular in Indian society, which is well informed about global trends and practices thanks to its free press, democratic system and familiarity with the English language, a national integrator. This is manifested in the series of Coke commercials that challenged the allegations of pesticides in Coca-Cola among other brands even when the JPC, with the help of top food scientists, was still investigating the matter. Ultimately, the final report condemned these commercials. This proved to be another setback for the company and the brand.

Fig. 1: Geographical distribution of volumes

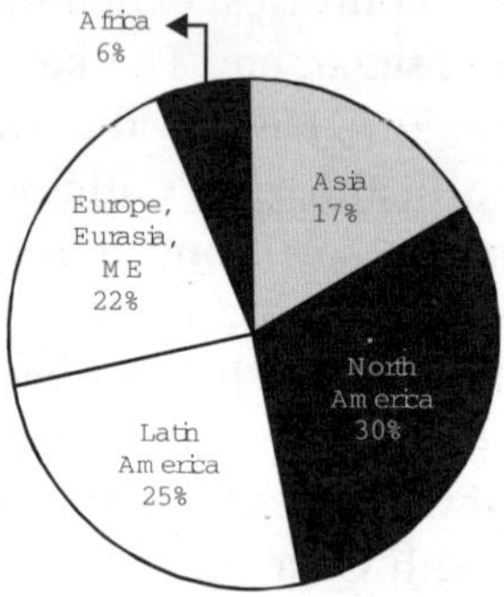

Source: TCCC Annual Report-2001

Fig. 2: Operating revenues

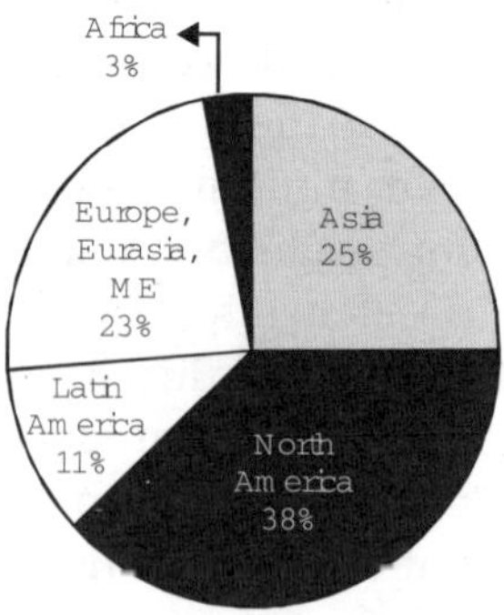

Source: TCCC Annual Report-2001

Fig. 3: Operating profit

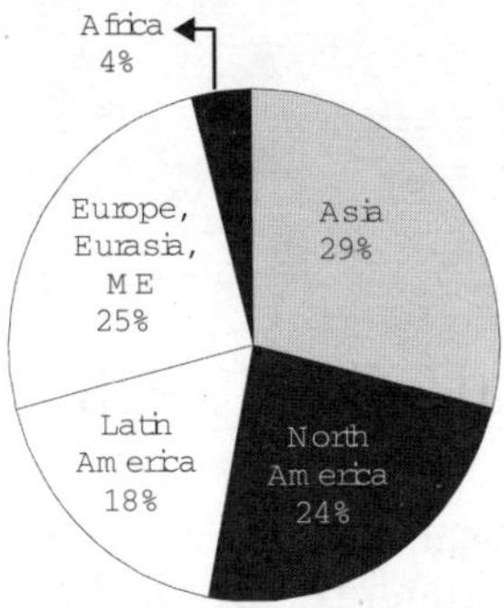

Source: TCCC Annual Report-2001

8

Think Local, Act Local

'Think Local, Act Local' is the first of the 'ten commandments' listed by Douglas N Daft, chairman and CEO of TCCC, before Christmas of 2000, in his *Red Book* 'renewing our promise for the 21st Century' for senior Coke executives and heads of groups, divisions and countries across the globe. The advice appeared to have been taken too seriously as well as literally by the Coke management to drive business growth in India. Many top Coke managers interpreted the idiom as 'when in Rome, do as the Romans do'. That seemed to have led to a lot of problems for the company in almost every part of the country, at operation centres and marketplaces, involving the Central and state governments, regulatory authorities, consumers and NGOs.

With a forward looking India going global, freeing restrictions on imports and foreign investments, lifting ceilings on executive remuneration and lowering corporate and personal income tax, the country expected global corporations operating in India to 'think global and act local' to ensure that they followed international practices at workplace and marketplace, manufactured standard products, respected local laws, local society, local community and acted like an ideal local company.

Unfortunately, Coke's behaviour was contrary to expectations as it used unorthodox means to tackle troubles. It also appeared as a possible troublemaker in its attempt to pursue a two-point business objective – drive volume and make money. Actually, India has long been an ideal ground for such entrepreneurs to succeed and thrive.

Indian laws and regulations concerning industry are not always very clear, encouraging various interpretations by entrepreneurs or businesses. For most industries, there is no single point regulatory authority. The country's federal structure provides the states with a lot of legal and regulatory powers with regard to industrial regulations alongside the Union laws and regulations. The 'grass root democracy' provides power even to local village level community administration to regulate industry and business. Therefore, there exists an enormous opportunity to manipulate the system and often get away with blue murder to achieve the ultimate business goal. Business manipulation was particularly common during the rigorous control-licence-permit-tax regime.

The soft drinks industry has been an ideal sector for entrepreneurs to perform the go-as-you-like act. Why should one follow strong and highly conscientious global practices in a country where local practices are so lax and underdefined? There are at least a dozen acts and regulatory authorities that govern the soft drinks industry in India. The ministries involved at the Union and state levels include Industry, Public Health, Food Processing, Water Resources and Environment, and Consumer Affairs. All of them have their own laws and regulations of which many of the existing ones are archaic. For instance, the present Prevention of Food Adulteration (PFA) Act, which defines soft drinks (carbonated water and sweetened aerated water), is of second World War vintage enacted by the administration of British India in 1945.

Despite the existence of such an elaborate definition, certain soft drinks brands created an impression that they contained juices because of their tastes and flavours. Therefore, one day the government came out with an order that manufacturers must ensure that they embossed the declaration 'contains no fruit' on all soft drinks bottles or containers from a specific date, allowing the industry reasonable time to implement the directive. Although the directive was several years old, Coke came in for a severe reprimand and its production and distribution units were randomly raided in 1993 with the threat to destroy tens of thousands of glass bottles which did not have the declaration printed on them. The company went to a high court to seek an injunction against such government action. There are instances of companies dodging such directives, which were issued when manufacturers followed 'local' ways to mislead consumers with wrong claims and practices.

For a long time, Indian manufacturers promoted bottled drinking water as 'mineral water'. The bulk packaged drinking water is sold in blue-tinted plastic jars instead of transparent white despite the directive against such a practice. They defend the sale of soft drinks after their expiry date for consumption by hiding behind another directive according to which the manufacturers are required to print on the bottles or containers 'best before date' or BBD in industry jargon. The BBD allows consumption of soft drinks within six months of their date of manufacture. However, the drinks could contaminate or change colour even before this date (BBD) if kept or displayed in the sun for weeks or months. Most small retail outlets do keep them out in the sun. The manufacturers are supposed to get BBD stocks collected after the date expires and destroy them under an established protocol. Few follow this established protocol as media reports of official raids of BBD stocks of brands like Coke would suggest.

Manufacturers always manage to strike a deal with regulatory or enforcement authorities whenever their ways are questioned or raids are conducted. Rules are bent and quality is compromised. In the end, nothing happens to the offenders and the consumers continue to suffer.

Companies are only sensitive to media reports. Negative stories, however correct they may be, must be stopped. If this is the way business operates in India, why should a company like Coke be any different? It would rather 'think local and act local' than follow global practices and go strictly by the international rulebook. In 2002, the resident editor of the New Delhi edition of *The Times of India*, the country's largest English language daily, called up Coke to find out if the company was actually using defective PET bottles for their beverages, after receiving complaints from an army officer's wife. It was reported that two large coke PET bottles purchased from the Army canteen in Delhi burst inside her car while she was driving. There were similar complaints of Coke's PET bottles bursting like missiles. Apparently, some of Coke's bottling plants were using poor quality PET preforms leading to these incidents. The practice was soon stopped. The company would never attempt to do such a thing in Europe, North America or Japan. In India, any compensation demand from aggrieved consumers is immediately branded as a 'blackmail' bid. The standard response to quality complaints is that the company follows TCCC's strict quality control and inspection regime, which leaves no room for complacency and mistake. The suggestion is that it could just be another spurious Coke bottle. Yet, consumer complaints pour in from every part of the country. And, they are nearly similar – burnt cigarette butts, tiny tobacco pouches, dust, nails, earthworms and even tiny reptiles inside the company's returnable glass bottles.

At the end of 2003, there were nearly 1,000 consumer complaints against Coke pending before various consumer courts in the country. Coke has an elaborate consumer response system, but few are ready to trust the company and are not prepared to hand over such bottles, their only evidence, to the company to conduct tests. They would rather visit a media establishment with their exhibits and show the contaminated bottle to reporters and photographers. In more advanced countries, this would have been regarded as a criminal offence and led to prosecution of top management personnel for slapping exemplary damages on the manufacturer. In India, the practice is to offer some free samples of drinks to complainants. If they refuse to accept, they are branded as ransom seekers.

If one of the purposes of globalization is to import global technologies and the best manufacturing practices to make the Indian industry efficient, price and quality competitive in the global market, the actions of companies like Coke should make the authorities think twice before clearing FDI proposals in such sectors that concern public health and environment. Coke and Pepsi's involvement in reckless painting of eco-sensitive Himalayan rocks along the River Beas near the picturesque Rohtang Pass was described as 'Rape of the Rock' by a national English daily, *The Indian Express*, which ran a campaign against the wrongdoings of the two MNCs and more so by Coke. The Solicitor General of India himself filed amicus curiae before the Supreme Court. The two companies along with others were made to deposit large sums with a court appointed body for restoration of the site. Ironically, the Chief Justice of the Supreme Court, who admitted the case, later sat on Coca-Cola India's first advisory board – created to deal with such controversies – to lead the company's environment council.

Coke may not be the world's most admired company, but it is certainly the world's largest brand, valued at US $70 billion in 2003. The value of a brand is all about its image and popularity. In India Coke is, however, better known for its adopting of the best practices at the workplace and marketplace. As if painting the Himalayan rocks was not bad enough, the picture of the trademark of Coca-Cola appeared in the front page of Delhi's *Hindustan Times,* one of the largest circulated English dailies in India's capital city, in September 2003, for spoiling the beauty of a heritage temple in another north Indian province in the serene Himalayan foothills. The picture showed that the brand was painted on an outer wall of an ancient temple. The Coca-Cola management reacted like any small-time local entrepreneur selling cheap brands. At first, it tried its best to get the news and picture 'killed'. But, after the newspaper front paged the story along with the picture of Coca-Cola signage, the company, far from being apologetic about it, sent a protest letter to the newspaper editor and owner, saying that the painting was done outside the boundary wall of the temple.

Coke acted local when it joined hands with other domestic manufacturers of packaged bulk drinking water, to scuttle a two-year-old government directive to the industry, asking it to replace the existing blue-tinted jars with colourless bulk jars for the benefit of consumers. Many of these bottlers do not follow very hygienic practices of jar washing and filling. With colourless and highly transparent jars the consumers could at least clearly see the inside condition of the jar and the water quality. Coke, an industry leader in the business of packaged drinking water, instead of joining hands with the government to instil greater consumer trust in its branded water Kinley, did what scores of other local operators selling cheap brands did for short-term financial gain. It lobbied strongly with the Ministry of Health and the Bureau of Indian Standards (BIS) alongside the other local manufacturers to get the directive either scuttled or its implementation deadline delayed. The Health Ministry ultimately agreed to extend the replacement deadline of blue-tinted polycarbonate bulk drinking water jars (containing more than 5 litres) by one more year till 31 July 2004. In the process, Coke saved a few millions of rupees in terms of replacement cost. The combined benefit to other members of the industry was much more. Indian consumers were the only losers.

Championing the cause of Coke's 'think local, act local' strategy are a few local satraps who had long been suggesting that expatriate managers are suspect in Indian society and cited examples of rival Pepsi and Hindustan Lever for their success. Such suggestions have no basis. Indian society has been habitually respectful and receptive to people and professionals from the West as well as the East, barring a short period when a self-help policy was pursued to support India's technologically outdated sick industry and build an inefficient public sector to take the country's economy to the brink of disaster. There are several examples of expatriate managers, including business leaders from GE, Siemens, Ford, Nestle, Samsung and LG, who are doing an exemplary job in the country and have ready access to any government department. What matters is the quality of the managers and their business practices. The propagation of such narrow ideas may benefit a few locals to fulfil their personal ambition, but it can also damage the image of a brand and the global reputation of its owners if the managers fight shy of deploying the best business practices for the sake of immediate results.

9

Coke and Controversy

Few companies have been so deeply mired in controversy over their sharp business practices as Coke in India. Some of them snowballed into major crises such as, the furore over pesticides in colas, over-exploitation and depletion of groundwater in Kerala, and dumping of industrial waste on farmlands, all of which attracted global media attention and prompted NGOs to rise in arms against Coke. There were also smaller controversies surrounding the brand that kept the local media busy every year. Coke's divestment fiasco, the environmental scandal triggered by Coke and Pepsi advertisements that was dubbed 'rape of the Himalayan rock', dumping of brand ambassadors Hrithik Roshan, Salman Khan and Sushmita Sen, all Bollywood stars, and the beginning of the water war in Kerala were the highlights of 2002. But the following year provided a deluge of non-stop entertainment for Coke watchers in the media and the public. Coke was constantly in the news for its wrong doings such as high pesticides content in its products, Islamic boycott in the wake of the Iraq war, dumping 'poisonous' sludge or waste water on farmland, 'sexual harassment' of a brand ambassador by a marketing top gun and the sale of BBD products in the market.

Even before the public interest in Coke's Himalayan rock painting scandal and divestment-dodging tactics died down, Coke was involved in a fresh controversy over the pesticides content in its packaged drinking water, Kinley, which became the country's No. 1 retail brand in 2002 displacing Bisleri, a former Parle brand and a market leader for 25 years. The Centre for Science and Environment (CSE), a well-known Delhi-based NGO with global connections, released a study of 17 popular packaged water brands, including Coke's Kinley, in Delhi, exposing alarming levels of pesticide residues in these bottled drinking water brands. The study was presented to the national and international media at a crowded press conference in India's capital city on 4 February 2003. Kinley faced the flak for being the worst among the four foreign brands that were tested. The three other brands were Nestle's Pure Life, PepsiCo's Aquafina and the imported Evian. CSE made the comparison of total organochlorines and total organo-phosphorus pesticide residues detected in these four foreign brands along with 13 other local brands vis-à-vis the maximum recommended limit for total pesticides prescribed under the European Economic Commission (EEC) norms. Expectedly, the fully imported Evian was the only brand that complied with the EEC norm for total pesticides (0.0005mg/l).

The fact that pesticide contamination level in bottled Bisleri water, the No. 2 brand in the market, was much higher than that in Kinley, Pure Life or Aquafina did not attract as much attention. Kinley and Aquafina boasted a combined share of over 50 per cent of India's retail packaged drinking water market. With Bisleri's market share being around 33 per cent at the time, other brands mattered little to the local consumers. The market had witnessed exponential growth – 40 to 50 per cent a year – after Coke entered the packaged drinking water scene. Coke marketed Kinley as the most trustworthy drinking water brand. The marketing strategy was an instant hit since drinking water quality in India has always been suspect. Waterborne diseases are most common in India. According to Professor Ramalinga Swamy, one of the country's reputed medical scientists and former head of the Indian Council for Medical Research, the poor quality of drinking water was responsible for 60 per cent of killer diseases and epidemics in India. These include cholera, typhoid, jaundice, various types of hepatitis, diarrhoea, dysentery and other intestinal diseases. Thanks to the green revolution there has been an indiscriminate use of nitrogenous fertilizers and a variety of pesticides (over 40 of them) for crop protection. The absence of a proper sewage system has heavily contaminated the groundwater in most parts of the country. Unfortunately, greedy soft drinks and packaged drinking water manufacturers rely mostly on groundwater as it comes free. Coca-Cola in India is no exception. There is a price tag for municipal water supplied or drawn for industrial use. Moreover, inefficient and underfunded municipal water supply departments in most states are unable to meet the daily minimum requirement of water for domestic consumption.

The quality of drinking water has been a matter of concern all over the world. Although the World Health Organization (WHO) has a common minimum standard for drinking water, advanced countries follow more stringent norms. EEC norms are probably the most stringent. Today, technologies are available to purify drinking water from pesticides contamination to the level of a particle per billion (ppb) or 0.001 per million (ppm). In India, the packaged drinking water norm existed only on paper till 1999 and manufacturers complied with it only on a voluntary basis. In other words, the industry was self-regulated. The changing lifestyle of Indian consumers, who are becoming increasingly health conscious, and the massive expansion of the bottled drinking water industry towards the end of the last decade, forced the government to re-examine the regulatory mechanism in order to control the mushrooming of bottled water manufacturers. The Union Health Ministry asked the BIS to get into the act. The quality norms fixed for bottled drinking water were on the lines of those recommended by the WHO. From 29 September 2000, BIS registration or certification was made mandatory for all manufacturers of packaged drinking water.

Under the BIS norms, the desirable limit for pesticides is given as 'absent'. The permissible limit is given as 0.001mg/l. The BIS norms for packaged drinking water and natural mineral water covered under the PFA say that pesticide residues 'should be below detectable limits' when tested according to the relevant methods. As many as 517 packaged water manufacturers, including six in the natural mineral water category, obtained BIS certification. Critics of BIS said that, although the bureau had provided standards for various physical and chemical parameters in the case of drinking water, these standards did not give maximum residue limits for individual pesticides. The standards for total pesticides were also not quantified. The limit 'below detectable level' was vague and ambiguous.

Worldwide, a lot of scientific research has been carried out on regulatory limits for pesticide residues in water. Of these, the one conducted by International Union of Pure and Applied Chemistry (IUPAC), Chemistry and Environment Division, Commission on Agrochemicals and the Environment, is very comprehensive and interesting. The IUPAC Commission's report on the subject prepared by an 11-member expert team made 12 recommendations for regulatory limits for pesticide residues in water. The experts represented some of the top internationally acclaimed scientific bodies and institutions from the US, Australia, Austria, Switzerland, the UK, New Zealand, Japan, the Netherlands, France and the Republic of China (Taiwan). Their recommendations are meant to act as 'a checklist for authorities introducing or revising limits or guidelines for pesticide residues in water'.

It is unlikely that the Government of India followed these guidelines while revising the regulatory limits for pesticide residues in water with effect from 1 January 2004. If so, the fault lay with companies like Coke, a global leader in the bottled drinking water business (TCCC's Dasani is among the most popular brands in the US) – as much as with the government – because of their enormous knowledge about the subject. Couldn't Coke set an example by producing the best quality bottled drinking water from the very beginning? Did it take the guideline levels of BIS or WHO, instead of the more stringent EEC, 'as a licence to degrade' its products to the guideline levels to keep the production cost low in order to take on local brands while setting to boost its volume and profitability?

The CSE report claimed that when tested for organochlorine pesticides and organophosphorus pesticides, the water bottled by the top five brands – Bisleri, Bailley (both Indian and owned by the Chauhan brothers of Parle fame), Kinley, Pure Life and Aquafina – and other less popular brands were found to be contaminated with these pesticide residues. The report said, 'among the organochlorines, HCH (lindane) and DDT were frequently detected. HCH was detected in 94 per cent of all samples. DDT was detected in 70.6 per cent of the samples. Metabolites of DDT like DDE and DDD were also detected. Endosulfan was present in 8.8 per cent of the samples. Among the organophosphorus pesticides, malathion and chlorpyrifos were most frequently detected in 85.3 per cent and 82.4 per cent of the samples respectively. People switch over from tap water to bottled water because they think it is not contaminated. The CSE laboratory test shows otherwise. 'Bottled water should not be considered a sustainable alternative to tap water. Source monitoring, reduction in use of pesticide and effective treatment seems to be the best choice for keeping a check on pesticide concentration in water', it said.

Coke's reaction to the NGO's report was predictable. In response, it launched a media advertisement campaign. It is another matter that Coke's print advertisement read more like a tender notice and was dumped with other assorted advertisements on the page to have little impact on the target audience, including the regulatory authorities. The key message of the Coke advertisement was: one could rely 100 per cent on Kinley's quality. In the end was the moral: '*Boond Boond Mein Vishwas*' in Hindi, which means 'trust in every drop'.

The government did not trust Coke's claims. Within weeks, it randomly raided and blacklisted several bottled drinking water manufacturing plants, including a few making Kinley. The report was all over the media. The copy was a joke even among journalists as it implied the company was 'welcoming' anyone to visit its international plants. Inside the company, the rumour was that it had been written personally by a senior executive of Coke's operations department, who saw himself as a great copywriter. It was unlikely that the company's internationally reputed advertisement firms or its Mumbai-based marketing department were involved in the exercise. Immediately after the CIS report, the company's statement to the media was that its water was free from any contamination whatsoever. It matched the highest international standards of the World Health Organization as well as BIS. Coke welcomed any further strengthening of quality standards. The government did not waste much time in strengthening the quality standards for the entire packaged drinking water industry. Within two weeks of CSE's press conference on pesticide residues in water, the government started working on an amendment of the PFA Rules, 1955, 'inviting objections and suggestions from all persons likely to be affected thereby before the expiry of a period of 30 days from the date on which the copies of the Official Gazette containing the said notification were made available to the public'. The matter was published in the official gazette on 19 February 2003 for the public to see. Rarely had the Government of India acted this fast on the basis of a public complaint.

The government received several suggestions and objections from the public, industry and trade associations during the 30-day notice period. Coke tried its best to see that the government soft-pedalled on the issue of forcing more stringent limits for pesticide residues in packaged drinking water. After a lot of consultations and deliberations, the Union Health Ministry decided to apply the EEC norms for bottled drinking water. The final notification was issued on 18 July 2003. It was signed by Deepak Gupta, a joint secretary in the Department of Health. The new norms were listed under the PFA (1st Amendment) Rules, 2003. The industry was allowed less than seven months to pull up its socks and bring about the necessary changes in the production process to become EEC rules compliant. Under the new rule No. 40, the notification made it very clear that '(i) Pesticide residues considered individually – Not more than 0.0001mg/litre (The analysis shall be conducted by using internationally established test methods meeting the residue limits specified herein) and (ii) Total pesticide residues – Not more than 0.0005mg/litre'.

It was bad news for Coke which had dozens of plants, including those belonging to franchisee bottlers and contract packers, across the country manufacturing Kinley water. It called for additional investment in upgraded technology and capital goods and a time-bound implementation. Ironically, a storm was brewing for Coke that would break within the next 18 days, about which it had no clue.

Yet, Coke seemed to refuse to learn. After the new quality standards for packaged drinking water on the lines of the European Union (EU) norms came into effect on 1 January 2004, the government issued a press note that said three Coca-Cola plants among several others were asked to shut down production of bottled water for failing to meet the new quality guidelines. The news was on the national wire service, Press Trust of India (PTI), and received wide media coverage all over the country. While Coke contested the news, its refutation of the official statement was wishy-washy. It said: 'all the products of The Coca-Cola Company, including Kinley drinking water, are totally safe. They meet all international and national norms on safety. The Coca-Cola Company has always met and will continue to meet all applicable laws in all countries, including India'. Soon after, Coke's 'new improved' packaged drinking water in India came for a price. The company raised the price of the bottled water by 20 per cent or more in many markets. So much for safety and 'beyond compliance' standards for Indian consumers! Back home in the US, it is another story. Bottled water prices have constantly moved downward. According to reports in the US, the pricing downdraft of bottled water had been swirling for several years and was expected to intensify in 2004.

While the pesticide issue kept Coke busy throughout 2003 fighting the NGO, the government, the regulatory authorities, the media and the public for 'justice', its corporate reputation was mauled by a new controversy involving the company's marketing head, Shripad Nadkarni, and a former 'Miss Universe' turned film actress, Sushmita Sen, brand ambassador for Thums Up, over an allegation of 'sexual harassment'. The news first broke in the media in early 2003, and it continued to appear periodically until the end of the year. The company denied any such harassment and its statement took shelter under the 'confidentiality clause' of the celebrity engagement contract. Coke's knee-jerk reaction to media queries with its statement, which often sounded more farcical than real, failed to impress the scribes. Infosys, India's most high-profile global company was faced with a somewhat similar situation when the head of its operations in the US, Phaneesh Murthy, was charged with 'sexual harassment' by a female colleague. The company came out in the open, spoke to the female associate, accepted a US $3 million blow for an out-of-court settlement, parted association with Murthy and made a full statement to the press. Infosys' ways were absolutely transparent and in keeping with its corporate image as the country's most admired company. If anything, the media supported the Infosys management. The incident disappeared from the print as fast as it appeared. In contrast, the Coke story remained a print media gossip for several months and titillated its readers. The final 'expose' came from *The Economic Times*, India's largest circulated financial daily, on 10 December 2003, which said Coke had bought Sushmita's silence for Rs 14.5 million (nearly US $330,000). The newspaper claimed that it was in possession of letters exchanged between Bachubhai Munim & Co., solicitors for the former Miss Universe, and Udwadia & Udeshi, Coke's lawyers. This made it 'explicit that the dispute between the two sides was indeed over the sexual harassment charge'. It was alleged that Coca-Cola terminated her contract on 23 February 2003 'because she had rejected the sexual overtures of a senior Coke official'. *The Economic Times* reported that Sushmita's solicitors said in a seven-page letter dated 7 April 2003 to TCCC's Chairman and CEO Douglas N Daft and the then India Division President Alex von Behr that the arrangement was terminated 'to punish Ms Sen [Sushmita] who rightly resisted sexual harassment by one of your employees based in the Mumbai office of Coca-Cola company'. It was said that the former beauty queen would identify her tormentor only if the India Division's head and/or a senior Coke official from Atlanta met her. Von Behr accompanied by India Division legal affairs Director Rajiv Sarin, met Sushmita at her Mumbai residence on 29 April 2003.

Going by the same newspaper report, the details of this meeting (29 April) are divergent, depending on whose version it is. Coke's solicitors, in their letter dated 29 July 2003, claim that Sen, apart from divulging Shripad Nadkarni's name, was only interested in 'extorting' money, and did not show any interest in von Behr's offer of an internal inquiry into the matter. They further denied all charges, and said that Coke owed her nothing, including Rs 5 million and Rs 4,785 of unpaid dues. Instead they made a counterclaim on Sen asking her to pay Rs 14.5 million for making false allegations. In response, Sen's solicitors sent another letter, dated 12 August 2003 – after the pesticides (in colas) controversy broke on 5 August – repudiating Coke's version of the meeting. They said Sen offered to give all details of the alleged sexual harassment before an independent enquiry committee. Von Behr had offered to set up an all female committee of Coke employees which did not inspire trust in Sen.

As for Coke's charge about Sen's extortionist behaviour, the letter said: 'These allegations and the threat of civil and criminal actions for alleged defamation are nothing but a show of might by an MNC in order to scare and muzzle our client'. The letter from Sen's solicitors added that 'in breach of the statutory responsibility and obligation Coca-Cola has proceeded to defend Shripad Nadkarni [...] It is ridiculous to even suggest that Nadkarni would admit to the charge of sexual harassment'. Sen's lawyers also claimed that she had told von Behr that 'a sum of Rs 14.5 million by way of compensation for sexual harassment should be paid by way of charity to an orphanage of our client's choice'. While Sushmita accepted Coke's offer to have the sexual harassment issue investigated by a former Supreme

Court Chief Justice S P Bharucha, the report said that Coke had paid the amount, Rs 14.5 million, to Sen and not to any charity.

Coke did not contest *The Economic Times* report. With the national and international media chasing Coke's India Division for its reaction to the story, the company's statement was typical: 'This is a dispute between a corporate and its brand ambassador with respect to celebrity engagement contract. Matter was discussed between the lawyers of both the sides. The same has been settled through a mutual contract between the company and Sushmita Sen for an agreed consideration. Both parties are bound by the confidentiality clause under the said contract. Contrary to speculative media reports, the consideration settled relates only to the terms of the celebrity engagement contract and bears no relation to the so-called allegation of harassment'. *The Economic Times* hit back after Coke's statement was put out by a national wire service, PTI, saying that it had all the documents in its possession 'to prove beyond doubt that it was this extreme charge [sexual harassment] which made the American soft-drink giant shell out the money' and the 'payment against the celebrity engagement contract is only a legal screen, deflecting attention from Ms Sen's sensational charge'.

The newspaper report, however, left many unanswered questions: Why did Sushmita take six long weeks after her contract was scrapped midway by Coke to level the harassment charges? Why did Coke terminate her contract? Did she originally agree to settle for a much smaller amount which the company was probably unwilling to pay? Was the sexual harassment allegation true or fabricated and designed to hit the world's largest brand where it hurt? Why did she ask and settle for such a small amount when she could have easily extracted much more? Why did Coke assign Nadkarni its marketing vice president, with greater responsibility after the whole incident without caring to wait for the investigation report from Justice Barucha? Is Justice Barucha's involvement real? What did the report say? Why did the company fail to envisage that the contract termination could cause trouble from her side and take preventive measures through proactive communication with the media about the termination and the reasons for it? Was the company's legal affairs director, who accompanied von Behr during his discussions with Sushmita and was deeply involved in the resolution of the issue, reinstated within days after he was officially released from the company? Did someone else from the company pay a private visit to Sushmita, long after Alex's visit, without the legal affairs director accompanying him? If so, why? Could someone benefit from Nadkarni's public embarrassment, as he remained 'guilty' until he proved himself 'innocent'?

Inside Coke, the Sushmita Sen story was a lot different and sounded more plausible. It said that Sushmita entered into a celebrity engagement contract with Coca-Cola India in February 2002 for a two-year term for an agreed consideration of Rs 15 million. The contract ran into trouble towards the end of that year when she allegedly failed to make herself available for a television commercial shoot in October and could not confirm dates again in December. This had upset Coke's Thums Up marketing plan. Following this, Coke sent a legal communication to the actress raising the relevant clauses in the contract. It was only after this notice that the contract was finally terminated in February and Coke asked the film star to refund Rs 10 million as damages towards the company's business loss. Sushmita's allegations of harassment and counterclaim of damages followed this communication. The 'sexual harassment' story was doing the rounds in the media in Mumbai as early as June 2003. Aaj Tak, India's premier television news channel, was the first to know about her charges of sexual harassment against Nadkarni and subsequent termination of her contract by Coke. The channel was persuaded to wait for a while for a correct version. However, the story broke on 30 June when almost all Mumbai-based newspapers approached Coke for its reaction. Coke's three-sentence statement given to the media was: 'There were some issues relating to the contract. Lawyers from both sides are talking and are in the process of settling the issue. We do not respond to rumours and speculation'.

Several newspapers and television channels reported the incident with Coke's evasive response. Later, Sushmita's lawyers also made similar comments to the media. Some senior executives of the company, including those from the marketing department, thought it was an opportunity for Coke to 'leak out' its correspondence with Sushmita before the termination of the contract to save the honour of the company and its marketing head. If this inside version of the Coke–Sushmita split was correct, an 'inspired media leak' of the development would have done immense good to protect its corporate image and the image of its head of marketing in India. The company was at the receiving end from the public, local and foreign media, national and international NGOs, national and state governments and regulatory authorities since the start of 2003 for a variety of 'wrongdoings'. If the company thought its huge advertising muscle could influence the media, it had made a serious error of judgement. Indian media houses, especially those owned by large groups, are absolutely free and operate in a highly competitive environment. In a free society, the media is rarely known to be supportive of government and high-profile corporates. India is no exception. Few trusted and paid attention to Coke's statements in the Sushmita case.

It is difficult to defend Coke's decision not to protect its corporate image and one of its key executives from such scandalous allegations if it had a true and reliable story to share with the public on such an incident. Some of the company's brand ambassadors from filmdom have been in the news for wrong reasons. The company and the brand Coke have been the worst sufferers. Rival Pepsi, which boasts a much bigger profile of brand ambassadors from both the film industry and the world of sports, has never faced such problems.

Towards the end of 2002, the company and the brand Coke received bad publicity, after its high-profile Thums Up brand ambassador, film star Salman Khan was arrested on charges of 'culpable homicide, not amounting to murder'. Khan had driven his Toyota Land Cruiser over five persons sleeping on a Mumbai footpath in the wee hours killing one person and seriously injuring four others. It was a hit-and-run accident and Khan was also charged with driving under the influence of alcohol. Khan spent many days in police as well as judicial custody. Every time his name appeared in the media in connection with the case, his association with Coke was featured. The actor had always featured on the edge of controversy because of his stormy relationships and escapades that ran foul of the law. He had been in trouble earlier when he was charged with killing a black buck in a reserve forest in Rajasthan in north India. Despite his somewhat tarnished image, Coke's 'Grow Up to Thums Up Challenge' campaign, featuring Salman Khan, was a huge marketing success in 2001. The campaign was run almost throughout the whole of 2002. It also saved Coke additional expenses towards on-the-ground brand promotion costs for Thums Up, the best Coke brand that appeared to grow on its own. Khan's engagement with Coca-Cola India expired on 31 December 2002.

Khan was once again at the centre of controversy in 2003, when brand Coca-Cola's new face, upcoming Mumbai film star Vivek Oberoi, alleged that he was receiving 'physical threats' from the former Thums Up brand ambassador for his reported affair with the most popular Coca-Cola brand endorser Aishwarya Rai, a former Miss World. According to film journals, Khan was 'obsessed' with Aishwarya and would not allow anyone to get close to her even though she 'rejected' him. Vivek Oberoi used the ceremonial launch of his first television commercial for Coke, which also featured Aishwarya, to tell media persons about the telephonic threats he had been receiving from Salman. Coke was holding a press conference at Mumbai's Oberoi Towers Hotel (now the Hilton Towers) for a preview of the television commercial. The new brand ambassador, Vivek Oberoi took the opportunity to speak to reporters on the sidelines during the lunch break and invited them to his residence the same afternoon. The result was predictable. Coke's television commercial launch got hardly any mention in the media, which ran big stories about the personal feud between the company's two brand endorsers involving the third. In the media and Mumbai's entertainment industry circles, the joke was a fight between mighty Coke and 'poor' Thums Up.

There was no winner. The only loser was Coke. The incident was more than embarrassing for the company. However, no one was pulled up for failing to warn Vivek before or after the press conference about talking to the media on that day on any subject, including his film career and personal life, other than the new Coke commercial and how he felt about his association with the world's largest brand. The trouble is the company seems to take everything and every situation for granted. Few can credit Coke with using its discretion when it comes to its image and reputation management. The management's decision and actions are driven by the aura of apparent invincibility of the brand.

Otherwise, why would Coke want to wade into a huge controversy by 'dumping' waste water from its plant at Varanasi in Uttar Pradesh on private farmland and then brazenly try to outface the public outcry. The situation, which turned pretty nasty following a prolonged civil unrest during the summer of 2003, could have been avoided if the company had only lived up to its promise to protect the environment. The narrow business objective of ramping up volumes and profits would appear to have overshadowed all other considerations. The Varanasi incident was a glaring example of how hollow Coke's oft-repeated 'concern for the community' really was. The Coke plant is located in the village of Mehdiganj, about 40 km from the holy city, surrounded by lush green fields and mango groves. The land alongside the Ganga, India's largest river with its source in the Himalayas, is very fertile and contributes substantially to the country's agricultural production of wheat, paddy, pulses and oilseeds. The plant is directly connected with a national highway that was being reconstructed. The two-lane road was being widened to four asphalt-coated lanes, under the care of the National Highway Authority of India. Work on the project started towards the end of 2002. The Coke plant is the only major industrial unit in the area that produces a lot of waste water. Before the reconstruction of the highway, the waste water used to pass through a small channel along the government land and a culvert under the road into a canal on the other side of the road before finally being dumped into the river Ganga. The highway expansion work blocked the culvert. As a result, there was no free outlet for the waste water discharged from the Coke plant. For months, this industrial waste accumulated along the highway and inundated several acres of private farmland. The stagnant frothy waste water bred mosquitoes. The stench spread far and near. The villagers demanded closure of the plant. Soon voluntary organizations, social activists and NGOs got into the act. The local media targeted Coke for damaging agriculture and environment in the area. Newspapers prominently printed pictures of farmland enveloped by Coke's factory waste and chemical froth. The company received a 'warning' from the Varanasi district administration and was ordered to take immediate measures to drain the accumulated water and clean up the place or face government action including closure of the plant.

The 'warning' worked. The company's 'incident management machinery' got into the act to 'manage' the government, highway supervisors, media and the community. Its operations team struck a deal with the contractors of the National Highway Authority to lay a metal pipe under the road to drain the plant's waste water into the canal on the other side of the road. Soon, some of the local village heads were seen 'aligned' with the company and said all good things about it to the state's chief minister and other important officers in the administration. Coke even promised a charitable health centre for the local people. The company's well-oiled incident management machinery had managed more difficult situations in other states. But, the party was spoilt when a baton-wielding police force outside the plant beat up anti-Coke demonstrators led by Magsaysay Award winner Sandip Pandey. The news and pictures of the police baton charge against the demonstrators were all over the local newspapers. Although the civil unrest against the company died down a few months later, the discontent among a large section of villagers continued to simmer.

A more careful Coke could have avoided the unpleasant developments at Varanasi if only it had tried to strike a deal with the highway building contractors to lay a pipeline below the road under construction before the culvert was closed. Possibly, the company took the poor semi-literate villagers for granted. Or maybe Coke thought any waste water clearance initiative could wait until the monsoon or even later so that the busy summer season production was not disrupted. Coke's Varanasi plant achieved record production in April–June 2003, to meet the massive summer demand for its products in the region. Rival Pepsi did not have a plant in the area. Coke did not appear to be repentant about the little discomfort it caused to the local community. It tried to deflect the blame on to the highway authority. The contractors could have stopped construction of the highway to build a new culvert at their own cost to help Coke run its plant without interruption during its peak business season. After all, the MNC had invested a lot of dollars to quench the parched throats of people in India with its famous fizzy drinks and, in the process, boost India's economy! Progress without patience and pain is rare.

The Indian public should know the global company's concern for environment, which is strongly stated in its *Red Book.* It says: 'A large part of our relationship with the world around us is our relationship with the physical world. While we have always sought to be sensitive to the environment, we must use our significant resources and capabilities to provide active leadership on environmental issues, particularly those relevant to our businesses'. Coke might have been accused of spoiling farmland with its industrial discharge in a poor, nondescript Indian village in Uttar Pradesh, but it contributes substantially to keep the South Pole free of solid wastes.

Coke's vulnerability to external attack was further exposed during this period from a rather unexpected source – India's 150-million strong Muslim community – even as the company continued to battle with hostile groups of NGOs, civil unrest in Kerala and Uttar Pradesh, a section of powerful politicians and bureaucrats in states and the Union and anti-MNC protests. Guided by mullahs and mosques, Muslim organizations play a very important role in determining the way of life of Indian Muslims in general, including their dress code, the type of education they should have, their political stance on local, national and international issues and even the food and drinks they consume. It has a strong political identity for its huge and often decisive voter base during national and state elections. Thanks to this huge strength of the Muslim vote bank, it receives strong support from some of the highly vocal secular, socialist and atheist communist cum ultra-Left parties. Therefore, it was no wonder that several

Islamic organizations in India with their massive following tried to exploit the situation arising from the American attack on Iraq in the summer of 2003 and issue a call for 'boycott' of US and British brands in India. While the 'boycott' call had little impact on the sales of most of the MNC brands, Coke, long regarded as an American icon, was specially targeted by the brotherhood for attack and the symbolic boycott in markets with a large Muslim consumer segment or in states with a large Muslim population and socialist or communist base.

Brand Coca-Cola has not been particularly popular in West Asian Muslim countries for many years, where rival Pepsi is more welcome. The distinctive brand Coca-Cola, read from right to left, is claimed to be blasphemous in Arabic. It is also supposed to have a Jewish origin. Anti-Coke campaigners often take advantage of such misinformation to arouse Islamic sentiments to press 'jehad' against the American brand. In India, they did it in the densely Muslim populated Lucknow, the capital of Uttar Pradesh, and some other parts of the state in 2001. However, the campaign died down after Coke's then vice president in charge of the company's public affairs and communications department, Irfan Khan, engaged a top Islamic scholar to issue a statement that there was no truth in such a mischievous interpretation. Irfan, himself a socialist and a former Hindustan Lever veteran, had a short association with Coca-Cola India. The Islamic boycott of Coke in the state of Kerala in the south-west fringe of India, was nearly total. In Kerala, the Muslim community comprises almost 33 per cent of the state's population. A large number of Kerala Muslims work in West Asian countries, including Iraq. Thousands of them had to leave their jobs in Arab countries to rush home in the wake of the

American military engagement in the region. They responded spontaneously to the 'boycott' call. The Left parties, which were in the opposition in the state's Legislative Assembly, soon joined hands with the Muslim community to make a lethal combination. They forced nearly 30,000 retail outlets in the state to stop the display and sale of Coca-Cola. They terrorized the trade by attacking Coke delivery vans, breaking and looting products and even hurling bombs at a godown of a prominent Coke distributor at Kochi, the commercial hub. The 'boycott' was partially successful in Muslim and Leftist dominated parts of other states like Andhra Pradesh, Maharashtra, West Bengal and Uttar Pradesh. Of them, West Bengal, where Coke has a number of plants, was ruled by a Marxist party-led Left coalition government. Coke was constantly in touch with the moderate section of Muslim and Left leaders as well as the bureaucracy in these states to minimize the impact of the 'boycott' and violent anti-Coke protests.

Fortunately for Coke, the movement against the company fizzled out by the end of July 2003. But the bad news for Coca-Cola is that for the first time in India its large Muslim population openly expressed their hatred for the brand although, maybe also for the first time, Coke's India team did not do anything silly to aggravate the situation. The global company, TCCC, was well-prepared to face such a situation to protect its business and assets in Islamic countries around the world and also those like India, with large Muslim populations. The global company had drafted strategies and tactics tailor-made for each of these countries and was constantly in touch with them to revisit these strategies and tactics on a regular basis. In India, Coke's public statement for external audience, including the champions of 'boycott', was that TCCC and its bottling partners were apolitical. They neither supported nor opposed governments or political causes. Violence and vandalism benefited none. Thousands of retailers, distributors and transport operators were being driven out of business because of boycott and threat of violence by a few. The government was losing revenue. Jobs of employees were becoming uncertain. The boycott of their products was not the appropriate way to further any cause. It only hurt the local economy, local business and local community.

While the low intensity 'boycott' blew over by end-July, Coke's India business received the biggest blow ever following a serious allegation against its product quality and its fitness for consumption that kept the entire company on tenterhooks till the end of January 2004, costing millions of dollars in losses in India operations and, worse still, acquired a new media-coined identity for its world famous brand: Pesticola.

10

Pesticola

New Delhi, 5 August 2003. It is a date that Coca-Cola India would wish had never appeared on its business calendar. The time was 11.30 a.m. The day was hot and sultry. The mercury had already crossed 36° Celsius. The weatherman had forecast that the temperature would cross 42° Celsius during the day, 4° Celsius above normal. August is the peak monsoon month in India, but there was no trace of a rain cloud over Delhi. This is the most ideal energy-sapping weather for outdoor sales of soft drinks. Market experience in India shows that the outdoor consumption of fizzy drinks is the highest at temperatures between 40° and 42° Celsius. Coke's Delhi sales team was already out in the market in full strength to push several thousand more cases into the system in a bid to ensure that the city's dehydrated millions kept reaching out for Coke products and did not have to opt for rival Pepsi's beverages because of shortages.

That was when the bombshell burst and all hell broke loose. The Centre for Science and Environment (CSE), an NGO, told a crowded press conference in Delhi that India-made Coca-Cola carried 45 times more pesticide residues than that was allowed in the EU. The pesticide content in Pepsi was 37 times higher. Ten other fizzy drinks brands manufactured by the two global cola giants in India had pesticide content exceeding EU norms by 11–70 times. The news spread like wildfire. Soon, it was beamed all over the country through hourly news bulletins on half-a-dozen national television channels and scores of regional language channels. Suddenly, it was a crisis of unbelievable magnitude. The cola business was about to lose its fizz. The head of Coke's India Division contacted the group office in Hong Kong and the principals in Atlanta. Almost bewildered, he contacted his counterpart in rival Pepsi.

It was a full-scale war – CSE versus the cola giants. The two cola supremos decided to jump into the trenches to fight the common enemy and address a joint press conference to snuff out CSE's allegations. A bitter war of words erupted between the NGO and the cola companies over the next six months, with Coke masterminding the cola brigade's moves and counter-moves. The Parliament of India, which was in session, stepped in to play its own role in the interest of public health. The Union and state governments also intervened. As the battle raged, it threw up opportunities for a range of politicians, seminarists, scientists, voluntary organizations, newspaper columnists and health freaks to further their own interests. With the country's parliamentary elections due in a year's time, the Right-wing political leadership in the government was in a flutter. There was an uproar in Parliament on 6 August with the opposition demanding immediate action against the cola companies and the country's highest legislature agreeing to ban the sale of fizzy drinks within its premises. The decision had a domino effect: the Indian armed forces halted sales of these soft drinks through their supply depots. The Parliament ban shook the confidence of cola consumers all over the country. If these products were perceived as health hazards for Members of Parliament (MPs), they could hardly be any less risky for their electorates. Coke's sales plunged overnight. The company had been in the eye of the storm for quite some time for one reason or the other. The Parliament sent soft drinks samples for tests to two of the government's best laboratories – one in Kolkata and the other in Bangalore to establish the veracity of CSE's claims. Several state governments took similar action, using their own laboratories or designated laboratories to confirm the allegations.

The Cola companies were put on public trial. The visceral antipathy towards arrogant MNCs showed through in the way that the newspapers and websites across the country handled 'the story of the year' with headlines that screamed 'Poison in your soft drink', 'Green study finds pesticides in colas', 'Colanisation's dirty dozen', and '*Cola dhanda becomes thanda*' (Cola catches cold). The Coke–Pepsi press conference, where they refuted CSE's allegations, received a minor mention in media reports. Coke may disagree, but many felt that the hurried press conference without adequate preparation and a clear strategy was a blunder for which the company paid heavily in the following months. The two cola company satraps hopped from one television studio to another to say: 'Look, that's bullshit [...] We follow much higher global standards. Our kids drink these products'. It was a childish argument and petulance was hardly the way to tackle the serious accusations. Expectedly, the television news channels did a clever job. They fielded CSE's firebrand director, Sunita Narain, against the Coca-Cola India head wherever he went to 'balance the story'. Tempers ran high, a top Coke official had a heated argument with a CNBC associate editor on the credibility of CSE's test report and the company refused to participate in the CNBC programme on the subject. CSE levelled two main charges: first, the soft drinks sold in India contained pesticide residues that was several times higher than the limits prescribed by the EU, and second that the MNCs were adopting double standards for their products – one for the US and Europe and the other (far inferior) for Indian consumers. Coke hit back at its detractors by seeking an independent scientific enquiry into the allegations of pesticide content in its products. The company said its drinks 'were safe and world class'. Coke's India Division chief said the company operated within European and American norms with 'top grade testing, top-grade products' and added that 'we have a strong set of regulations internally and externally'. 'Our products are tested in "gold standard" laboratories in Hyderabad and the Netherlands'. The company also tried to rubbish the CSE charges by saying the NGO did not have the expertise to conduct such sophisticated tests. The BIS – India's standards-setting body – was not impressed with the company's offensive. *The Times of India* quoted the government agency on the same day as saying that they would 'apply stricter rules for bottled water to the raw water used for soft drinks'.

What did the CSE say? The NGO said that it had picked up three bottles each of 12 soft drink brands including Coca-Cola, Fanta, Sprite, Limca and Thums Up, and tested them at its state-of-the-art laboratory. The tests revealed that all the soft drink brands contained a cocktail of deadly pesticides far exceeding the permissible limits in the EU. The NGO also said these products did not breach Indian laws which were 'weak or non-existent' for all practical purposes. In contrast, the sample bottles collected from the US 'showed no trace of pesticides'. It said both the US and Europe had established standards and rules under which citizens could drag companies to court if they flouted regulations. The CSE tests established high individual pesticide residues in the local samples: an average of 15 times higher for DDT and metabolites; 21 times higher for lindane; 42 times higher for chlorpyrifos; and 87 times higher for malathion.

The CSE was highly critical about the Indian government's regulatory norms. 'This is worse than the bottled water case. At least mandatory certification is needed for the bottled water, but there is nothing for this food (soft drinks) industry'. The NGO said the rules on arsenic levels in soft drinks allowed 0.5 ppm (parts per million) while the BIS said it should be 0.25 ppm. The limit for bottled drinking water was 0.05 ppm. That means 'you [manufacturers] are legally allowed 50 times more arsenic in soft drinks than in bottled water', it said and added that the same went for lead, copper and cadmium. The Cola giants tried to debunk CSE's allegations by arguing that its laboratory was not accredited. But that was also true for one of the government labs – Central Food Laboratory (CFL), Kolkata – to which the government sent soft drink samples for testing after the storm over pesticide laced colas erupted. A body called the National Accreditation Board for Testing and Calibration for Laboratories (NABL) certifies the capabilities of establishments to carry out such tests. NABL, however, is a voluntary third party accreditation programme and laboratories are under no compulsion to seek accreditation. But here is the irony: while the government did not insist on accreditation of the laboratories, the government's own

Department of Science and Technology (DST) said it would accept the test results submitted by institutions that carry out tests on products which are in the international marketplace only if these were from accredited laboratories. Coke claimed that its soft drinks were tested at an accredited laboratory in Hyderabad as well as those in the Netherlands and the US and further added to the parliamentary committee investigating the commotion over 'spiked' soft drinks that 'no laboratory in India has been accredited for analysing soft drinks'.

The CSE said its Pollution Monitoring Laboratory was modern and well-equipped to carry out the tests. 'The laboratory aims to bring science out into the public domain; it undertakes scientific studies to generate public awareness about food, water and air contamination. It is equipped with state-of-the-art equipment to monitor and analyse air, water and food contamination. It has high performance liquid chromatograph (HPLC), gas chromatograph (EC) with various detectors, UV-VIS spectrophotometer, mercury analyser and respirable dust sampler among others. The laboratory provides scientific services at nominal cost to communities that cannot obtain scientific proof of local pollution. Given the state of scientific research in India – most of it restricted to national defence and food security – the laboratory is an effort to use science to achieve ecological security.'

The conclusions derived from the CSE laboratory analysis of the soft drinks samples were:

- Out of the 16 organochlorines, 12 organophosphorus and four synthetic pyrethroid analysed from soft drinks samples, lindane, DDT and its metabolites, malathion and Clorpyrifos were most commonly found in 36 soft drinks samples tested.

- Lindane, a potent carcinogen, was detected in 100 per cent of the samples analysed. The average concentration detected in all the samples was 0.0021 mg/l, which is 21 times higher than the EU limit for individual pesticides. Lindane is the most toxic of all the isomers of HCH (exachlorocyclohexane) and has powerful properties and is used for the control of insects of field crops and pests in houses.
- DDT was detected in 81 per cent of the samples analysed. The average concentration of total DDT in all the samples was 0.0015 mg/l, which is 15 times higher than the European Union limit.
- Chlorpyrifos, a suspected neuroterratogen, was detected in 100 per cent of the 36 samples analysed with an average concentration of 0.0042 mg/l, which is 42 times higher than the prescribed EU limit.
- Malathion was present in 97 per cent of the samples analysed with an average concentration of 0.0087, which is 87 times higher than the EU limit. Malathion was present in all samples except Sprite.
- The average concentration of total organochlorines was 0.0038 mg/l, that of total organophosphorus was 0.0129 mg/l and the level of pesticides detected was 0.0168 mg/l, which is 34 times higher than the prescribed EU limit. The variation in different bands could be due to the different ingredients present in different brands, composition of pH.
- No pesticide residues were detected in the Coca-Cola and Pepsi samples from the US manufactured by the same multinationals.

Highlighting the impact that pesticides could have on human health, the CSE report said: 'Lindane is absorbed through respiratory, digestive or cutaneous routes. It accumulates in fat tissues. It damages liver, kidney neural and immune systems and induces birth defects, cancer and death. Treatment with 1–40 mg of lindane per kg of body weight disrupts testicular morphology, decreases spermatogenesis, inhibits testicular steriodogensis, reduces plasma androgen concentrations and may adversely affect reproductive performance in males. In females, lindane disrupts the estrous cycle, reduces serum estrogen and progesterone levels and sexual receptivity. Chronic exposure to lindane has been linked to an increase in the risk of cancer of the aerodigestive tract and strong genotoxic effects on tonsillar epithelium. It also affects the excitable membranes and the cardio-circulatory system. DDT is linked to a decrease in semen quality and increased risk of breast cancer in women, spontaneous abortion and reduced bone mineral density. DDT and its metabolites, because of their lipophilicity and long half lives, accumulate in the food chain. Chronic exposure to Chlorpyrifos has been shown to cause immunological change. Chlorpyrifos toxicity becomes acute if transformed to chlorpyrifos oxon, which is a potent anticholine esterase, 1000 times more toxic than chlorpyrifos. Chlorination is commonly used for treatment of domestic water supplies which is a new concern. Malathion affects the nervous system. High exposure can cause respiratory paralysis and death'.

The CSE disclosures sparked a near panic among all concerned. Union Health Minister Sushma Swaraj announced in the Parliament that the samples of these soft drinks would be tested independently and separately in two government-owned scientific institutions – CFL, Kolkata, and CFL at the Central Food Technological Research Institute (CFTRI), Mysore. The soft drink samples were sent by the Directorate General of Health

Services, New Delhi, to these laboratories for analysis of pesticide residues. The samples collected and sent to these labs were from four plants.

With Parliament already having given a 'thumbs down' to Coke and Pepsi's soft drinks brands, Coke had more reasons to worry because of a fresh development in Kerala regarding the quality of sludge generated at its plant. The Pollution Control Board (PCB) of Kerala found dangerous levels of cadmium, a metallic chemical that can cause cancer, in the sludge generated at the company's plant in the state. The board issued a press release on 6 August 2003, barely 24 hours after the CSE's sensational announcement of pesticides in colas.

Coke had a humongous crisis on its hands – and its core team of managers needed to display deft crisis management skills to deal with it. After the infantile arguments it had marshalled at the joint press conference and the petulance shown by the top honchos on television shows, it continued with its ham-handed approach. It came out with a long-winded advertisement in newspapers the next morning to assert the quality standard of its soft drinks. The headline of the advertisement read: 'Coca-Cola manufactures World Class & Safe products in India'. It was followed by a shoulder message and a rule drawn below to look like a small box on top of the box carrying the text message. Never mind the bad design, layout and a boring copy, even its visibility was poor because of the positioning of the black-and-white advertisement in some newspapers.

As on the previous occasion, this time too Coke did not appear to have taken professional help from its marketing department or the local creative thinkers from its famous international advertisement agencies while drafting this important message. The shoulder of the somewhat amateurish copy blared: 'The *most valuable* brand in the world makes no compromises on the quality of beverages it serves the Indian Consumers' [Italics denote emphasis in the advertisement]. Did the India Division management take Atlanta's permission to use the two emphasized words 'most valuable'? Several months later, a parliamentary report had punctured several of the India Division's tall claims. Why drag the global brand's equity to protect the questionable quality of a product meant for the local market? The Division would probably have done well to 'think local and act local' under such unusual circumstances.

All these didn't work. Coke's third quarter sales figures in India showed that very few, if any, took its advertisement and the company's safety statement displayed outside retail outlets at face value. Within days Coke's men from the Hong Kong group office were in Delhi to personally assess the situation. The key message was: manage Parliament, manage ministers and manage media. We don't want this to go out of hand. One of them was even heard saying rather desperately 'if the situation so demands, we will pull out of this country'. It was an unusual situation for Coke, the like of which it had not experienced anywhere in the world. After its Belgium experience, where it faced a ban after the carbon dioxide controversy, Coke was expected to be more careful about its products and operational style. So panicked was the management that a senior executive from Hong Kong attending a presentation of Coca-Cola India's new citizenship project, Bharat Jal Kosh, at Delhi's five-star Maurya Sheraton, drove out two senior members of the public Affairs and communications department and asked them to be in Parliament to 'manage' members at 9.15 a.m. Obviously, these people had funny ideas and perceptions about India. To them, everything in India appeared to be 'manageable' with money and connections. One may argue it wasn't Coke's fault that the Indian government's standards and inspection regime were not as strict as they were in some other parts of the world – and it was merely exploiting a loophole. Moreover, India's consumer movement is as weak as the government's regulatory system. There is also a strong duality in the approach of the administration and the public in dealing with different entities – local and external.

It took almost a fortnight for the government laboratories in Kolkata and Mysore, to test the samples collected by the government for pesticide residues and to submit the results to the Union Health Ministry. This was probably one of Coke's most agonizing fortnights in India. Coke had gone through the dog days earlier – when it planned its re-entry, squabbled with bottlers over their buyout, dithered over divestment or during the trial before the Supreme Court – but this was something unprecedented. As soon as the test results reached Delhi, Union Health Minister Sushma Swaraj made the announcement in Parliament bringing a great relief for Coke and Pepsi. Surprisingly, the minister's statement left out a very important observation by CFTRI, Mysore, which said, 'As the samples analysed at CFL, CFTRI, Mysore, was entirely from a different batch than the CSE samples, the results obtained are not comparable with the results of CSE'. This observation is very significant and holds the key to the pesticide contamination of groundwater in India. The CSE samples were collected in May 2003 or during India's peak summer cropping season. Farmers use irrigation water to grow high-yielding summer crops. The consumption of soil nutrients and pesticides is the highest during this season. The incidence of groundwater contamination under farmlands or adjoining areas by pesticides is generally very high during this season. However, the soft drinks samples sent by the Directorate General of Health Services for pesticide residue tests to the CFL, Kolkata, and CFL–CFTRI, Mysore, were collected in August 2003, in the midst of the country's peak monsoon season. During this period of the year, the consumption of pesticides is generally very low. The underground availability of water increases substantially. This significantly reduces pesticide concentration in groundwater during this period. The peak business season for soft drinks and bottled drinking water in India lasts for four months – from the middle of March to the middle of July. This could be another reason for the variation in test results between the government-owned and CSE laboratories. Not only were the batch numbers of the samples different, but also the gap between the collection dates of these samples was significantly long (three months or more), making the respective residue test results incomparable. Moreover, variations in any analytical research are a well-known factor. This important point gets only a passing reference in the CFL–CFTRI report and in the Joint Parliamentary Committee (JPC) report. Later, two other laboratories – one belonging to the government's Central Pollution Control Board (CPCB) and the other a well-known private entity, Shriram Laboratory, tested soft drink samples. While the results of the CPCB test came close to the findings of the two other government labs, Shriram Laboratory, which tested one sample each of Coca-Cola and Pepsi, found the pesticides residue percentage in both the products 'quite high'. Six months after CSE's disclosure of high pesticide content in India-made colas, the JPC report clearly mentioned that the committee found CSE findings to be correct on the presence of pesticide residues in carbonated water strictly in respect of the 36 samples of 12 brand names analysed by them. After this, Coke's loud assertion that it serves uniform international quality products in India is put under a serious question mark.

Both Coke and Pepsi went gaga over the minister's statement in Parliament on 21 August 2003, calling it a great victory for them on the pesticides issue. As soon as the minister completed her statement in Parliament, Coke's India Division head positioned himself in a suite at Delhi's Taj Mahal Hotel on Man Singh Road to give a series of media interviews to drive home the key message – The company's position had been fully vindicated. The minister had given it a 'clean chit'. The products were totally safe and met all national and international standards. All major television channels, national and regional newspapers and international wire service agencies were invited one after another to meet the company's India business boss and to get his reaction to the minister's statement. The exercise lasted for almost eight hours. A senior executive team from the group office at Hong Kong was present in another suite in the same hotel monitoring television coverage of the minister's statement, public reaction and the India head's performance before television cameras.

Coke carried an advertisement the next day claiming the minister had given a 'clean chit' to its products. These instant 'clean chit' claims by the soft drinks manufacturers enraged the opposition members in Parliament. Some of them accused the government and the health minister of having struck an 'understanding' with the two giant MNCs and demanded a joint parliamentary probe into the pesticides allegation. An embarrassed and visibly upset health minister snubbed Pepsi at a press meet for making a false claim in the advertisement and demanded a public apology on the 'clean chit' issue. She also accepted the opposition demand for the setting up of a JPC to investigate the whole issue of pesticides in soft drinks. Thus, Coke would appear to be partly responsible for the creation of the JPC and thereby, prolonging the issue. As an industry leader with a 60 per cent market share, the company could have been a little more patient and refrained from interpreting the minister's statement in a manner that would spare her and the government from embarrassment. Coke could have convinced Pepsi to follow a common strategy on reacting to the minister's statement. After all, both the companies were constantly in touch with each other on the issue of pesticides, sharing technical information and using the same public platform to trash the NGO's allegations. The JPC was like a carbuncle on elephantiasis, forcing Coke to go on the offensive and trying to mould public opinion, manage the perception of JPC members, political parties, bureaucrats and the trade bodies, scientific community, bureaucrats, farm lobby among others. The company was in the forefront in this prolonged exercise while the rival Pepsi decided to lie a bit low this time and concentrate more on marketplace activity to slowly restore consumer confidence through constant visibility and increase its sales volume.

Between 6 and 21 August 2003, Coke's India Division launched a massive campaign vilifying the CSE report. The company was even getting ready to launch criminal proceedings against CSE. On the advice of the group's legal head from Japan, who had come down to India to take stock of the situation, the India Division, however, filed a civil suit against Sunita Narain in the Delhi High Court, which was subsequently withdrawn at the instance of the court. Coke sent out hundreds of letters to MPs, union ministers, state chief ministers and other ministers, and senior bureaucrats. Hard copies of a PowerPoint presentation were shared with and explained to the editorial management of most major national dailies and television news channels and also some of the country's highly influential regional newspapers. All regional directors of Coca-Cola India were asked to conduct this exercise in their respective regions. The original idea of the 'myth versus reality' docket was, however, Pepsi's to suit its business, which went beyond selling beverages. Pepsi's international snack foods business (Frito Lay) is a big business in India as well. In addition, it is a big exporter of India's agri-products. Therefore, Pepsi's presentation gave a new twist to CSE's allegations suggesting that they were part of a bigger EU agenda to erect non-tariff barriers against India's agri-products exports. Pepsi's CEO in India himself went about communicating this fear to the media and the government. Coke's India Division also bought this line and championed the cause of the country's agriculture in its external communications for PepsiCo India's benefit.

Pepsi did a very clever job, which greatly helped in broad basing the issue of pesticides in water encompassing the country's entire agriculture sector and food processing industry. Newspapers devoted thousands of columns' centimetres on pesticides content in farm products, including fruits, vegetables and milk, and processed products like juices, tea, coffee and sugar. The campaign appeared to be a big hit as a new pesticides scare permeated India's entire farm sector, which produces food grains, cash crops, oilseeds, pulses and commodities worth over 400 million tonnes a year to feed the country's huge human and animal population as well as for pisciculture. The campaign, as desired, created more confusion for the government and the entire nation. Coke's India division can certainly claim a fare share of the success of the Pepsi-led otherwise hilarious 'pesticides-everywhere' campaign. It was scary as well as entertaining, watering down CSE's pesticides in soft drinks report to a large extent.

The Coke campaign also darkly hinted at similar motives behind the idea of championing the cause of EU standards. It said it would possibly permit European water companies a competitive advantage under General Agreement on Tariffs and Trade (GATT) in India's domestic market. It also raised uncomfortable questions: 'Could EU norms be a market tool, focused on their commercial interests rather than human health and safety, or should we adopt EU norms for other categories too apart from water, like environment, labour, human rights, food, pharmaceuticals, law, FDI, trade unions, NGOs, etc., or, have they (EU norms) been prepared via a transparent and participatory process?'. It said 'Codex Alimentarius and WHO are internationally accepted guidelines based on food safety'.

Initially, it appeared that Coke's campaign against the implementation of EU norms and its efforts to discredit the CSE report did not go in vain. The company impressed upon a number of trade and industry associations like the Confederation of Indian Industry (CII), Federation of Indian Chambers of Commerce and Industry (FICCI) and Associated Chambers of Commerce and Industry (ASSOCHAM), of which the company is a prominent member, to take up its cause with the government. Later, CII and FICCI made a big issue of the credibility of the CSE report, especially the fact that the NGO's laboratory was not accredited to NABL.

Meanwhile, several high-profile NGOs, local as well as international, continued to gun for Coke in India. The heads of these NGOs have strong media and political links. They also have their own journals and websites, which people read and trust for their less political and non-commercial views. Several of them are media columnists and command greater respect in society than commercial organizations. Coke's campaign evoked a series of media interviews of the CSE director, Sunita Narain, all over the country to keep the controversy alive. *The Times of India* carried an interview with the CSE director on 12 August 2003, on the edit page that was designed to blunt the counter criticism of the NGO report. When asked on the motives behind the CSE report, Narain said: 'We checked for pesticides in bottled cold drinks being manufactured and sold in the US and found they were all pesticide free. But when the same tests were conducted on bottled soft drinks sold in India, we found high levels of pesticides content [...] This speaks volumes for double standards being employed by global companies. We are asking the government to tighten regulation on companies irrespective of their size and power'. On the pesticide contamination of groundwater, she said, 'There is no governmental control whatsoever on the use of groundwater. So much so, that the companies, which are making huge profits in the country, are accessing our groundwater resources completely free of charge. Surely, the government should have by now made it mandatory for companies to pay for the water they use'. The CSE director called for a policy that ensured safer use of pesticides. CSE insisted on more stringent EU guidelines than the WHO norms as 'there are no Indian guidelines on the subject. There are three sets of international guidelines – from US FDA, WHO and EU. We did not opt to use the first two because they do not cover all the pesticide residues'. The NGO was critical about the government's lackadaisical attitude towards the safer use of pesticides. 'Globally, we have come to learn that if a certain pesticide or chemical is opposed and phased out, then it is usually replaced, under another label, by an equally harmful pesticide. The way forward is to make companies liable for damages. Unfortunately, there has been no response from the government so far. And our findings are being seen as a battle between us and the industry, which it is not'.

On 22 August 2003, a motion was adopted in the Lok Sabha (lower house of Parliament) for the appointment of a 15-member JPC, consisting of ten members from the Lok Sabha and five from the Rajya Sabha (upper house). Political parties from both the ruling coalition and the opposition were represented in the committee. The JPC was asked to establish 'whether the recent findings of Centre for Science and Environment (CSE) regarding pesticide residues in soft drinks are correct or not' and 'to suggest criteria for evolving suitable safety standards for soft drinks, fruit juice and other beverages where water is the main constituent'. Opposition leader and former Defence Minister Sharad Pawar, the senior-most member of the committee, was named as the chairman of JPC. The latter was mandated to submit its report to Parliament 'by the beginning of the winter session' which meant within three months. However, the JPC sought and obtained the Parliament's permission for some more time to submit the report towards the end of February 2004, when India's annual national budget session starts. The report was finally presented to the Lok Sabha on 4 February 2004, and was laid on the table of the Rajya Sabha on the same day. The normal budget session was postponed as the country decided to advance the national elections by several months. The JPC involved some of the country's top scientific resource persons in the concerned fields like Dr G Thyagarajan, Dr N P Agnihotri and Dr S K Khanna in preparing the report and drawing conclusions. Dr Thyagarajan was appointed as a full-time consultant to the committee. Dr Agnihotri and Dr Khanna worked part-time. Interestingly, Coke had no appetite for waiting this long to launch a television commercial offensive to restore consumer confidence in its products, especially after the sample tests conducted by the governments of Maharashtra, Gujarat, Rajasthan and Kerala and independent national and international labs found the company's product samples met the required safety standards. The Coke commercials, which emphasized the fact that the product had been certified 'safe' by national and international testing laboratories, did not go down well with the JPC members and many others.

The JPC proceedings revealed some very interesting facts about the bottled water and cola business in India. For instance, the Association of Indian Bottled Water Manufacturers told the JPC that the cost of processing water was very low – about two to four paise (per litre), including standardization of the product. While the JPC report carried excerpts from the presentations made by industry, corporates, trade associations, autonomous institutions, scientific bodies and relevant government departments, the committee probably did not have enough time to cross-check the information provided by the two soft drink manufacturers. This could be because of the sudden change in the country's political climate towards the start of December 2003, following reports that the BJP-led National Democratic Alliance would go for an early national election. Most MPs, including the JPC members, were preoccupied with their preparations for the elections since a lot more was at stake for them in the polls than the JPC report, which anyway would be considered only in the next Lok Sabha. The immediate concern was their respective party organizations, poll alliances, nominations and keeping close contact with the constituencies. There were inconsistencies, if not contradictions, about the way the two companies responded to the same set of questions. The legal departments of these companies made sure that their individual responses were loaded with dry technical stuff with a lot of references to their global knowledge and experience. Coke submitted a very long response, often repetitive and forceful. If anything, it revealed details about the company's vast experience in dealing with governments and public institutions all over the world, especially in developing countries, over several decades. Such long-winded reports could be quite boring for generalists, which most politicians are. Coke was extremely critical about the proposal to set standards for pesticide residues in water based on the EU norms for soft drinks. Coke's note to the committee on the health ministry's proposed standards for soft drinks and standards for soft drinks in other countries said: The proposed standards on pesticide residues do not follow the guidelines for setting standards for foods as per Codex Alimentarius. Worldwide standards are made only on agricultural commodities and not on finished products. Standards should be based on sound science and risk analysis. The above standard is not based on scientific risk assessment nor does it consider any generally applied risk analysis principles. This proposed standard is based on EC regulation for pesticides in potable water that is not even intended for multi-ingredient foods like soft drinks in Europe, only to the water used in the manufacture of foods and beverages. Soft drinks contain other ingredients in addition to water, such as sugar and other plant-derived materials that are permitted to contain acceptable levels of pesticide residues. The European norm for water was based on technical limit of quantification and it was recognized that not all countries will be able to meet this level of quantification. It is generally understood that product containing agricultural ingredients such as sugar and juice cannot be regulated as water.

Coke's answer to the JPC was that the common standard followed by all countries is that water used in soft drinks and other processed food industries should be of the same standard as that laid down for drinking water. It is well accepted worldwide that agricultural ingredients like sugar and juice may contain low levels of pesticides exempting soft drinks from the same regulations as applied to water. The presence of ingredients other than water in soft drinks makes it virtually impossible to accurately determine the pesticide residue levels. It suggested that the government should establish maximum residue limits (MRL) for farm products and raw agricultural commodities (RAC), and implement good agricultural practices to resolve the matter at the grass-root level.

Incidentally, Pepsi's note to the JPC on the same issue said it all in just three easily digestible sentences without the effrontery of trying to lecture the Indian government on GAP, development of food law and its application.

Coke received a questionnaire from the Lok Sabha Secretariat on 11 December 2003. The somewhat innocent looking questions did not give the impression that the committee's back office had enough time to do proper homework about these companies, their operational style, including employment of contract packers, purchase of water through contractors, dealing with consumer and community complaints and the number and nature of these complaints. The JPC also relied a great deal on the honesty of these companies and it probably expected them to make voluntary disclosures. In the process, it played into the hands of these companies which managed to convert specific micro issues, like the high pesticide content in India-made foreign brands and their dual quality, into a macro issue of pesticides menace in agriculture. Given the time constraint and the complexity of the issue, the JPC cannot be faulted for some of these lapses. The report had to be filed within the first week of January 2004 after which the Lok Sabha would be dissolved. If it failed to do so, the next government would consider the whole matter afresh and constitute a new JPC for the purpose.

The JPC raised several points for Coke to respond. In addition, a separate list of six specific points in the form of questions was attached. The questions were:

- Standards followed by companies across countries and are they different in India?
- What are the quality systems followed in India versus the rest of the world?
- What are the details of your water purification process?
- What has the company done after the controversy to ensure that their products are safe?
- What should be the process of setting standards in India?
- How is your concentrate manufactured in India? How do you test various ingredients for certification? How are imports handled?

A similar list and set of questions were also sent to PepsiCo India for its response. Both Coca-Cola and PepsiCo vehemently opposed the setting of Indian standards for bottled drinking water and soft drinks and pleaded that the standards for water used for manufacturing soft drinks should be based on WHO guidelines for water. PepsiCo also said that the companies did not check the quality of sugar which was added to soft drinks though they did their best to procure the best quality of sugar available.

In its oral evidence, the CSE insisted that it chose the EU norms as it was the cheapest to implement in this country. The CSE also insisted that stringent measures had to be put in place and standards for soft drinks should be set on the basis of the MRLs of the ingredients so as to not endanger public health. In a subsequent note, CSE put its views more precisely. It said: 'As there is no MRL standard for sugarcane (hence sugar) for DDT, lindane, chlorpyrifos, malathion in the Indian law, that is, the Prevention of Food Adulteration Act or even in EU standards or USEPA or

Codex, there can be no acceptable limit for these pesticides in sugar'. If the scientists and ministries were not united about the fixing of standards for soft drinks, the industry contradicted itself on a vital point raised by CSE about the manufacturers using groundwater free. Coca-Cola India said emphatically that 'The water is not free. At all the manufacturing facilities we pay water cess charges. Also numbers of units are being charged for water from irrigation department and industrial development corporation'.

Coke produced a list of 29 bottled water plants that applied for registration with the Central Ground Water Authority (CGWA) along with the registration fee paid. Of these, seven plants did not require registration fee. The fee itself was a pittance, mostly varying from Rs 1,000 to Rs 2,000 per borewell all connected with high capacity electrically operated pumps. What about Coke's other beverage manufacturing units? Water cess and the CGWA registration fees are not the same thing. The cess is on the quantity of the water drawn from underground resources within a plant, which can be instrumentally measured. All industrial water supplies from government or municipal sources are levied. Increasingly, even domestic consumers of municipal water are required to pay tax.

Pepsi was a little cleverer in its response. It said the company had 15 operational bottling plants throughout the country. It had taken 'required approvals from the concerned authorities for use of water in the manufacturing soft drinks and is paying water charges as applicable'. However, the Association of Indian Bottled Water Manufacturers provided the last laugh. The Association, a much larger representative body, told the JPC that the manufacturers were not paying any charges for using groundwater. 'No, there is no charge. Nobody has asked for it', the association said. When asked whether permission was taken from the Gram Panchayat (village administration) for drawing groundwater, the association representative said: 'No sir. But in some places you are required to have the permission for digging borewells, like in Mumbai where you have to take the permission of the Municipal Corporation. I do not know about other places whether the permission is required or not'.

Although it was possible that the association representative deposing before the JPC was not fully knowledgeable about the position of water cess in all parts of the country, the statement by the top bureaucrat (secretary) in the Ministry of Water Resources was rather shocking, especially in the light of what Coke had told the committee. He said that the government charged no money for this purpose. Secondly, the statutory position about the ownership of the groundwater was this: whoever has the land is the owner of the water which can be extracted from the land. That is the position of the Act. If an agriculturist takes out water from his land, it is his land. The government has nothing to do with it. The bureaucrat's viewpoint is his own. Not many in the government, judiciary, academic circles, social activists or even politicians will agree with him. The government may be doing 'nothing' about it now, but it will come under pressure to do something sooner or later to stop reckless exploitation of groundwater which affects the whole society. From population control to drinking water availability, everything is political fodder in India and vote linked. That explains why farmers, the biggest single influencer of ballots, are so pampered in India. The fertilizer they use is subsidized by the Union government or the whole nation; the electricity they consume to run pump sets is subsidized by state governments. The diesel they use is subsidized by the Union government. The use of underground water is free. The water they use from irrigation canals is as good as free. Yet, the agricultural income of the country's farmers, which accounts for almost 50 per cent of India's Gross Domestic Product (GDP), attracts no income tax. Fortunately, things are changing – though at a snail's pace.

States are under pressure from the World Bank, which has been pumping in a lot of money to support the generation and distribution programmes of India's highly fund starved power sector, to do away with the electricity subsidy for farmers. It is only a matter of time before the government starts taxing the users of underground water, especially for industrial purpose. A social movement is already gaining ground against free exploitation of groundwater by industry since the community has to bear the cost and suffer from water depletion and shortage. Coca-Cola is already under fire for overexploitation of groundwater at a number of locations causing hardship to the local community. Unfortunately, neither the Union Ministry of Water Resources nor the state governments have done enough to address the growing public concern about the free use of underground water by industry.

In a half-hearted admission, the secretary to the Ministry of Water Resources said that commercial use of groundwater in water scarce areas needed to be regulated and a levy might be fixed sometime in the future. That was his personal opinion and not the ministry's. He said 80 per cent of the country's drinking water needs were being met from groundwater. The rest came from the surface water. The central legislation on the use of groundwater for industrial or agricultural purposes and fixing levy on such uses is practically impossible.

Under the country's federal structure, groundwater figures on the State List of the Indian Constitution, states alone can enact legislation for use of groundwater. The Indian Parliament can make laws to regulate or control the development of groundwater in states only with their request and consent. However, a few states and Union territories have their own laws pertaining to the use of groundwater. They include the governments of Goa, Tamil Nadu, Lakshadweep, Pondicherry, Kerala and Andhra Pradesh.

In Gujarat, the State government has set up a groundwater authority for control and regulation of groundwater resources in the state. The Andhra Pradesh Water, Land and Tree Act, 2002 came into effect from April 2002. The subject is relevant to understand the operations of water-based companies like Coca-Cola. CSE's campaign against 'pesticides in soft drinks' has pointed out that the multinational cola giants could spend a little more money on purification of their products since they are freely tapping the groundwater inside their plants. The Coca-Cola system in India has the largest number of plants. Almost all of them have electrically operated deep borewells inside the plants to meet most of their water requirements. In the face of statements made by the Association of Indian Bottled Water Manufacturers and the union Ministry of Water Resources and the legal position explained by the union Law Ministry, Coke's bold submission under oath before JPC that 'the water is not free and all our manufacturing facilities pay water cess charges' would appear to be far from the truth.

Referring to the effect of pesticides in soft drinks on health, the CSE also mentioned the adverse impact on health of other ingredients like caffeine, artificial low-calorie sweeteners like aspartame, saccharin, ascesulfame-K, sugar, acids and carbon dioxide. Regarding caffeine, CSE said, 'A methylated xanthine, caffeine is a mildly addictive stimulant drug, used in soft drinks as a so-called "flavouring agent" [...] Large amounts of caffeine consumption can cause diseases and disorders such as insomnia, nervousness, anxiety, irritability and deviations from the normal heart rate. A major concern about caffeine is that it increases the excretion of calcium in urine, which increases the risk for osteoporosis in heavy caffeine consumers. Some epidemiological studies correlate exposure to caffeine during pregnancy to the occurrence of congenital malformations, fatal growth retardation, miscarriages (spontaneous abortion), behavioural effects and maternal fertility problems. The ill-effects of caffeine can be gauged by the fact that the US FDA (US Food & Drug Administration) issued an advisory in 1981 warning that "pregnant woman should avoid caffeine-containing foods and drugs, if possible, or consume them only sparingly". The US FDA still maintains that advisory as its official policy'. CSE also said: 'Low-calorie sweeteners are non-sugar substances that are added to food and drink products instead of sugar. They have sweetness many times greater than conventional sugar. Artificial sweeteners like saccharine, aspartame and acesulfame-K have been linked to numerous diseases like cancer increasingly'. On sugar, the CSE statement said, 'The average bottle of soft drink (300 ml) contains about 15 grams of sugar, if we follow the specifications of soft drink quality given by the FPO. That is five teaspoons of sugar. It is highly unlikely that an average individual would eat five teaspoons of sugar at a time everyday, and eat it more than once a day. But by consuming soft drinks, that's exactly what we end up doing. It is well documented that diets high in refined sugar promote obesity, which increases the risks of diabetes, high blood pressure, stroke, and heart disease. Sugary soft drinks also promote tooth decay. The high sugar content is a major reason why health professionals are concerned about frequent consumption of soft drinks'.

On the ill effect of acids and carbon dioxide on human health, CSE submitted that 'dentists around the world are reporting complete loss of the enamel in the front teeth in teenaged boys and girls, who habitually drink soft drinks. The culprit is phosphoric acid in soft drinks, which causes tooth rot, as well as digestive problems and bone loss. Phosphoric acid has also been associated with calcium loss and kidney stones in numerous medical studies. Acid drinks increase dentin permeability by opening dentinal tubules leaving a dentin surface completely uncovered and removing the smear layer. Dental cavities are often associated with consumption of carbonated beverages because the amount of sugars that are consumed is important in forming caries caused by the bacteria mutans streptococci, which is a part of dental plaque. Lactobacillus and actinomyces viscosus are two other kinds of bacteria that adversely affect teeth and survive well in very acidic environments, produce high amounts of acid from sugars and other types of acids. A common problem that is associated with the consumption of large quantity of soft drinks is the increased acid levels throughout the body causing gastronomic distress due to the inflammation of stomach and erosion of stomach lining leading to painful stomach ache as the stomach, which maintains a very delicate acid-alkaline balance, can be set out of balance by the consumption of a large number of soft drinks, which can create a constant acid state leading to indigestion and gassiness'.

Whatever be the points of view of the cola companies on the effect of the ingredients in the soft drinks on the human body system, there are more scientific papers against these drinks than in favour of them. Therefore, the safety aspect cannot be ignored. The key issues are the consumption level, the addiction level and the age and lifestyle of the consumers. A status paper of the National Institute of Nutrition under the title 'Impact of Long Term Consumption of Pesticide Residues on Health in India: Issues Needing Further Research' is also an interesting reference material. The JPC report also refers to this status paper. In essence, this is somewhat similar to what CSE has mentioned. The health concerns include reproduction disorders in women, chronic nervous system effects, cancer risk, impaired lactation and oestrogenic effects.

On the issue of the caffeine risk, Coke was asked by JPC to give reason for selling non-caffeinated soft drink in the US and Europe while it sold caffeinated soft drinks in India. Coke contested such a notion and stated that 'the per capita consumption of soft drinks in the US and Europe are many folds higher than in India. The company conducts market research to find out the preference and needs of the consumers and develop products to suit the consumer needs. Based on such needs the company had launched non-caffeinated products in countries like the US and Europe. However, the caffeinated products continue to have very high demand and the decaffeinated sale is less than 10 per cent because caffeine in our product is used as a flavour. Based on the consumer research, Coca-Cola India had also launched Diet Coke in India. Currently the sales of Diet Coke are less that 0.5 per cent of total sales. Our consumer research studies do not indicate the need for such products in the near future. The Coca-Cola Company sells caffeinated soft drinks in every country in which we do business, including the US and all countries in Europe. Caffeine-free cola products are sold in some countries, because market research has shown that a significant number of consumers want the choice between caffeinated and caffeine-free versions of some of our cola products. If consumers in India show a significant interest in caffeine-free cola products, then these products will be offered in India along with caffeinated cola products. We do provide several non-caffeinated soft drinks in India such as Limca, Sprite and Maaza. Caffeine is not a harmful or "high risk" food ingredient. According to a comprehensive review recently conducted by Canadian health officials "the possibility that caffeine ingestion adversely affects human health was investigated based on the review of (primarily) published human studies obtained through a comprehensive literature search. Based on the data reviewed, it is concluded that for the healthy adult population, moderate daily caffeine intake as dose levels up to 400 mg per day [...] is not associated with adverse effects such as general toxicity, cardiovascular effects, effects on bone status and calcium balance (with consumption of adequate calcium), changes in adult behaviour, increased incidence of cancer and effects on male fertility".

Besides caffeine, the JPC appeared to be concerned about several newspaper reports on the quality of Coke products in the market, sale of products without the manufacturing or expiry date and other consumer complaints. The committee sent an additional list of points on 7 January 2004 and wanted a reply from Coke within 48 hours. It also quizzed Coke on why 'Switzerland does not permit phosphoric acid in the soft drinks manufactured in that country'. The other questions were related to water and pollution.

In the end, nothing much came out of the JPC report. It was not expected either because of several factors such as time constraints, the sudden political development arising from an early Lok Sabha election, the vastness of the subject and all inclusive terms of reference, lack of validation of various claims by companies and government departments. A sense of frustration might have also influenced some of the members of the committee with regard to the fate of such a report submitted just before the end of the term of a Lok Sabha. Many JPC reports on several critical issues have been gathering dust in the Parliament archives. The report had something for every concerned player in the business. It will not be easy for any government to implement the committee's recommendations within any short period of time, except for things like matching the EU norm for bottled water as well as soft drinks and the declaration of caffeine content in the coloured soft drinks. The report did not recommend any punitive action against offenders, especially in view of growing complaints of product quality and undesirable operational practices with regard to the sale of BBD products, defective packaging and unscientific packaging. It may be because it was not specifically mentioned in the committee's terms of reference. The committee's report was an eye-opener at least in one area – the lack of concern of the government and regulatory authorities for public health.

The committee made several 'Observations/Conclusions/ Recommendations' on the issue of pesticides. The committee was of the view that so far as the quantitative aspect is concerned, CSE findings were 'correct on the presence of pesticide residues in carbonated water in respect of three samples each of 12 branded products of Coca-Cola and Pepsico analyzed by them'.

Coke's (also PepsiCo's) bid to derail the government's initiative to fix new standards for soft drinks by widening the issue of pesticides to cover all ready-to-serve (RTS) beverages, including juices, tea, coffee and agro-products proved to be futile as the JPC thought it was too sensitive an area for tens of millions of farmers, small self-employed traders and vendors and the common man to be treated at par with the fizzy drinks. The JPC report clearly stated that 'fruit juice and other ready-to-serve beverages have nutritional value. The soft drinks market is dominated by two global giants with access to state-of-the-art technologies and techniques and thus would be expected to show the way to better food safety. Fruit juices and beverages are primarily in the small and medium sectors and are labour intensive. There are millions of fruit and vegetable farmers who provide the raw materials and thus constitute a principal support base to the fruit juice and beverages units. Given the current levels of pesticide residues allowed in raw fruits and vegetables, and given the socio-economic ground realities, the fruit juices and beverages industry needs to be treated differently compared to the carbonated water sector. The same standards cannot apply to them equally. Pesticide residues in food are a phenomena related to agricultural practices as they enter the soil and plant systems and work their way into the food chain. It is not a manufacture related issue and, therefore, it will not be fair or proper to apply the carbonated water and packaged water (pesticide) residue levels to the fruits and vegetable juices and such beverages'. The JPC recommended that 'standards notified under draft notification for pesticide residue should not be made applicable for fruit juice and other beverages'. The question is: will this recommendation apply to Coke's popular juice-based RTS drink Maaza, India's largest juice brand? If yes, it will come as a major consolation to Coke. It will also boost the company's future plans to introduce other juice brands or products in India. Maaza's market share in its category is close to 40 per cent. Coke is the largest industrial consumer of mango pulp which is used in the production of Maaza (a mango-flavoured drink). Mango is a farm product.

The JPC was scathing in its comments about the quality of potable water and the lack of official concern about it. Obviously, the committee was not aware of the practices or malpractices followed by even some of the top MNCs in the bottled drinking water business under the 'watchful' eyes of the regulators in the US and Europe. As recently as in March 2004, Coca-Cola was accused of 'using ordinary tap water as the source of its fancy brand (Dasani)' sold in the UK market. The sensational revelation was made by Britain's top newspapers *The Daily Telegraph, The Times* and *The Guardian. The Daily Telegraph* said the company used the tap water supply to its factory in Sidcup, south-east England, as the source for its bottled water Dasani, a top US brand which had recently been introduced in the UK market. *The Times,* London, reported that Coca-Cola had put a designer price of 95 pence (1.4 euros or US $1.7 or nearly Rs 80) for 500 millilitres of bottled Dasani water. The British water company Thames Water charges only a fraction (0.0316 pence) for the same amount of its processed water through the tap. Thanks to the international wire service agency, the news is now in public knowledge all over the world. Coke explained that its water goes through a 'highly sophisticated purification process'. One 'stage, called reverse osmosis, is described as a technique perfected by Nasa to purify fluids on spacecraft'. Such pompous statements are ridiculous. The technology is so common and inexpensive that the cost of processing water even in India is said to be as low as two paise per litre. And, most of the India's innumerable bottled water manufacturers use the reverse osmosis process. A company spokesperson told the *The Daily Telegraph* that 'the point is quality rather than provenance'. The British water industry said the product's (Dasani) implication seemed to be that local tap water was impure. Barrie Clarke, spokesman for Water UK, which represents suppliers said: 'We don't think there are any impurities in tap water. People don't need to buy this stuff to get excellent quality, healthy water'.

In the light of such reports coming from a country like the UK, known for its highly stringent quality standards for foods, beverages and water, one only wished that JPC spent more time to re-examine some of the claims and statements made by the manufacturers such as Coke. In all fairness, the JPC members, however, working under severe pressure created by an impending national election and their own political future, did not succumb to pressure from the industry and its 'supporters' in the government. The JPC had repeatedly cast aspersion on the inadequacy of the existing laws and incompetence of various departments to regulate the industry. It pointed out that 'it is only recently that when the CSE brought out a report on 4 February 2003, with respect to the presence of pesticides in some samples of bottled water and highlighted the hazardous effects of such pesticides on human health in their report, that the Technical Committee of BIS thought of convening an urgent meeting and recommended new standards. These standards were ultimately notified by The Ministry of Health and Family Welfare […] dated 18 July 2003, and have already been implemented *w.e.f.* 1 January 2004. The limits prescribed for individual pesticides have now been prescribed at 0.0001 mg/litre and for total pesticides, it is 0.0005 per litre'. The JPC may not be entirely right to give all the credit to CSE for the bottled water controversy. The impurity in the bottled water was brought to light at least four years ago by a Gujarat-based NGO, fighting for consumer rights, which was also publicized in the media. But few paid much attention to it.

The JPC report, if anything, proved that there was substance in the 'allegations' of CSE and Coke was on a weak ground in trying to resist any attempt to fix higher standards for its soft drinks. The six-month long parliamentary hearing on the pesticides issue did not help improve either the corporate image of Coca-Cola in India or its brand image. Few will accept its 'Clear Hai' (It's safe) advertisements even in good humour after the JPC report was officially released. The ill-advised battle against the NGO has exposed to the parliamentarians and the public several new fronts of its operational practices, all of which are potential crisis points and could attract government or legislature level investigations. This will provide new grounds for powerful anti-MNC NGOs to fight companies like Coca-Cola to stop commercial exploitation of the earth's most scarce and valuable resource – drinking water.

The JPC report was leaked out to the media in piecemeal by some of the committee members, before it was tabled in both the houses of Parliament. It was a clever attempt by the MPs to make sure that the public got to know all critical observations and recommendations of the committee in instalments, day after day. The release of the whole report in one day would have had much less impact. CSE's Sunita Narain had the last laugh. The showdown benefited the NGO immensely by establishing its credibility and a sustained year-long publicity through the national and international media since its first report on pesticide contamination in the bottled drinking water was released in February 2003. It also had a significant impact on consumer awareness of the safety aspect of soft drinks. Coca-Cola felt that the JPC appreciated the CSE's role in bringing out in the public the entire pesticide issue in the food chain. It was, however, critical about CSE for not getting its results validated or scientifically assessed by an accredited lab.

The JPC came down heavily on the Central government for its 'knee-jerk' reaction in setting up draft notification on the lines of EU norms. The Health Ministry worked without circumspection and discretion causing panic amongst the public. The JPC recommended adoption of Codex norms and the highest norms for quality of water being used in making CSD. The JPC appreciated the steps taken by the industry for using the hot carbon treatment for purification of sugar. The Committee took a positive view of KO initiative in recharging groundwater. PepsiCo was 'chastised' for its lack of initiative on this front. The JPC appreciated KO's commitment to quality standards in respect of its franchise operations and was concerned that PepsiCo washed its hands off the responsibility for the product quality of its franchisees.

If the media coverage of JPC's final report along with its 'Observations, Recommendations and Conclusions' was any indication of the public mood, the headlines in all major newspapers across the country on 5 February 2004, said it all. *The Times of India* carried the story on the front page with a four-column headline, which said 'Cola mein kuchh kala: JPC', meaning there was something fishy in cola. The report said the Union government had been told to fix norms for soft drinks and to clean up its act on water safety. The front page headline in the *Hindustan Times* said: 'CSE got it right, colas have pesticides: JPC'. *The Economic Times* ran the story under the headline: 'JPC asks government how it can be soft on soft drinks sector'. The news was carried with a picture of a disgusted looking Britney Spears at the premiere of Pepsi's new TV commercial with a caption 'Even She'd Agree'. It said that JPC wanted food standards and strict regulation of the Rs 6,000 crore industry. *Business Standard* said: 'JPC final report confirms pesticide residues in colas'. *The Hindu Business Line* said: 'JPC report upholds CSE findings'. *The Indian Express* headline was a direct hit at the cola companies. It said: 'Hard rules haunt soft drinks'. *The Statesman* headline cried: 'JPC nails "germ colas" says they're unfit for kids'. *The Hindu* said: 'JPC confirms pesticides in cola'. Almost all major vernacular newspapers front paged the JPC report with headlines suggesting that the cola bluff had been exposed. Coke's reaction to the JPC report – saying 'our products manufactured in India are world class and safe. Our products already meet the science-based norms recommended by the JPC' – was mentioned briefly in all news reports as a matter of routine. Even the international media gave wide coverage to the JPC report with similar headlines. *The Washington Post* headline said: 'Pepsi, Coke Censured in India. Report Confirms Pesticide Findings of Environmental Group'. Coke's reaction quoting the company's Asia spokesman David Cox was somewhat different and conciliatory. Said Cox: 'We are happy to have this dialogue about quality that would move toward building confidence of consumers, as long as it is based on scientific findings by accredited laboratories'. Cox had flown down to Delhi all the way from Hong Kong to give his reaction to Delhi-based foreign media correspondents. Coke is rarely comfortable with the India Division's communication skills when it comes to dealing with the foreign media. The entire Public Affairs and Communications team of Coke's group office in Hong Kong along with the company's international media consultants camped in Delhi for several days after the CSE blew the whistle on pesticides in colas. The parent company's concern and embarrassment over the issue was understandable.

The India crisis came almost close on the heels of the Belgium crisis over product quality involving the carbon dioxide content in Coca-Cola and the poor storage condition. *The Financial Times* headline was short and on target. It said: 'Indian pesticide-in-drinks claim upheld'. The international wire service, Reuters' story went under the caption 'Indian lawmakers uphold pesticide report on Colas'. The Agence France Presse (AFP) despatch was filed under the headline 'Coke, Pepsi sold in India contain pesticide residues, says parliamentary report'. Most of the foreign newspapers and agencies carried reasonably long stories on the JPC report to merit three to four-column headlines. Reuters' story quoted Coke as saying 'whatever standards the government concludes are the most appropriate [...]' This was different from Coke's statement to AFP, which said 'our products manufactured in India are world-class and safe. We follow one quality system across the world'. *The Financial Times* report carried an interesting remark by Coca-Cola India's advertising adviser saying 'this is a classic case of cheap populism which does a disservice to the Indian consumer. Most of India's drinking water is unfit for human consumption but the politicians have found it more convenient to go for the global brand names'. It was an uncharacteristically bold reaction on the part of Coke to justify pesticides in its cola on the ground that the free municipal supply of tap water was anyway 'unfit for human consumption'.

Is there any lesson for Coca-Cola India from the pesticides controversy? 'There is. And, the most important one is that we should project ourselves as an Indian company and not an American multinational', said a key member of the company's local management team, which seriously believes that with some genuine efforts its American origin and parentage can be whitewashed from the minds of Indian consumers. Was he echoing the company's local advertising adviser's line? One couldn't be too sure. Of late, the company has been trying hard to wear a populist mask that would hide its American connections and project itself as an Indian firm to attract local sympathy or appreciation. After all, local firms or local brands do get away with so much more wrongdoings.

Shortly after Coke's last expatriate CEO left the India Division to head the company's Philippines business, a puja was reportedly performed in 'the corner room' of Coca-Cola India's corporate office at Gurgaon, near Delhi, apparently to drive away the evil foreign spirit which might still be hovering around the place. After the puja, sweets were offered to all Coke employees at the company's cafeteria. Maybe, it was a first step towards Indianization of the mighty American MNC. Unless the employees themselves believe that they work for an Indian company and Indian brand, they are unlikely to be most effective in their communication with consumers to spread the message. There could not have been a more innovative and radical way to strengthen an employee's belief in the desirable corporate and brand image of the company than a Hindu priest coming and offering puja chanting Vedic hymns right in the corner office of the India headquarters of Coke, which is credited with the creation and marketing of the Christian world's most modern icon, Santa Claus in red.

Will Coke be able to convince the powerful NGOs and activists and the likes of Sunita Narain, Vandana Shiva, Magasaysay award winners Medha Patkar, Sandip Pandey, Rajendra Singh (nicknamed 'Waterman of India'), media baron M P Veerendrakumar and writer Arundhati Roy that this is a desi (local) cola? Sounds funny. But there is nothing wrong in trying to change the perception of the public, including these respectable personalities, having a huge following all over the country. They are the ones who have been campaigning against the commercial exploitation of water by companies like Coke and fouling the environment. India, in Coke's own admission, is not a great nation for soft drink consumers. With the company spending millions of dollars in advertisements and television commercials to promote its brands, it could soon be one. That is the worry of these activists, environmentalists and social thinkers. It is probably true that there is no way Coke can strike a chord with these powerful women and men, working with their feet on the ground for the benefit of the country's tens of millions of underprivileged, undernourished and famished people, to smoothly drive its business. Maybe, Coke feels that while it tries to win over the common man, politicians, bureaucrats and others with its 'Indian company' spiel and a more visible corporate citizenship programme, it can isolate the handful of potential problem makers and take them head-on. Coke seems to believe that such tactics were bound to succeed in the long run. Its no-holds barred approach to malign CSE is only one such example although it failed to achieve the desired objective for the present.

Coke hardly paid any heed to CSE's first report on pesticides in bottled drinking water. A senior Coke official boasted that he knew about CSE's investigation into the impurities in the packaged drinking water almost two months before the results were announced. The company did nothing to improve the water quality to protect its soft drinks from a similar NGO ambush attack. It did not try to work with the NGO to deal with the problem of pesticide contamination of water and its impact on soft drinks, if any, to defuse the issue. Instead, the company was all out to publicly discredit the NGO, discount its technical competence and question its intentions. Ultimately, the company was forced to implement the EU norms for bottled drinking water in all its plants within 11 months of the CSE report under a government order to avoid being 'blacklisted'. And, all this fuss for a processing cost of two to four paise per litre! Seasoned corporate watchers, however, feel that the company is treading a dangerous path which any sensible business enterprise anywhere in the world will wish to avoid, leave alone in an extremely vibrant democracy like India. Unfortunately, Coke may not be fully aware of the dangers of adopting confrontationist tactics against its critics.

11

Water Thief

There are times when money brings out the worst in people: it leads to bad judgement, forces one to act on half-baked information, formulate unclear strategies, devise unethical practices, adopt questionable tactics and become arrogant. This applies to cash-rich corporate organizations as well as their managers. Money corrupts corporate behaviour and judgement. Coke's decision to set up a water plant in a rain shadow area in Kerala is just another instance of poor judgement.

Plachimada village in Kerala's Palakkad district was perhaps not the right choice for the location of a beverage plant since it depended so heavily on underground water reserves. The tribal village is right in the middle of a rain shadow area. The rainfall beyond the radius of 20 km from the plant is almost normal, but not where the Coca-Cola unit is located. Rainfall at Plachimada is far less compared to the average rainfall in the state of Kerala. Plachimada's green surroundings are highly deceptive. It belies the underneath truth – lack of rain and an acute drinking water shortage in the area. One can't blame the water-starved local community for accusing Coca-Cola of stealing their water to make millions of cases of beverages at its plant for commercial gains.

The plant started commercial operations in March 2000. Within a year, Coke's relationship soured with the local community, the village administration, NGOs, Leftist groups, student organizations, tribal bodies, anti-MNC protesters and the state's second largest newspaper group, Mathrubhumi. The company faced a sudden backlash from different people and organizations. It was soon fighting one of its worst battles in India to ensure the survival of its Kerala plant. The stakes were too high for Coke and it could not afford to do anything stupid. If these activists managed to kick Coke out of Kerala, it would have a domino effect in other parts of the country that were also facing an acute water shortage. For reasons best known to Coke, the company had decided to establish its bottled water plants in several dry and arid areas.

In one sense, the Plachimada crisis was Coke's own creation. If the company had carried out a proper feasibility study by an agency familiar with the local sociopolitical situation, it would have probably been advised to avoid not only Plachimada but the state itself. The controversy over the state of groundwater reserves at Plachimada, stemmed from three burning questions: whether or not the aquifer supporting Coke's operations was independent of other aquifers; whether or not Coke was over-exploiting the aquifer; and whether or not Coke was responsible for the water scarcity in the area.

Kerala is unique in many ways. The country's greenest state is situated along the narrow ridge of the Western Ghats in the east, on the one side, and the Arabian Sea in the west, on the other. The tiny southern state of India is on the international eco-tourism map; often described as 'God's Own Country', Kerala opened its doors to Christianity as early as AD 52 when St Thomas, one of Jesus Christ's 12 direct disciples, first landed on its shores. Muslims came a few centuries later as traders and not invaders as in the case in the north-western part of India. Today, Kerala's population is divided almost equally among the three principal religious groups – Christians, Muslims and Hindus.

In the last six decades, the state has given the leadership to the country's socialist movement. It boasted of the first democratically elected socialist government as early as the 1950s. Kerala has also been a home for environmentalists and strong Leftist trade union movements. Kerala is also a strong base for NGOs. No industrial project, that has undermined the state's environment or run foul of its militant trade unions, has been known to survive in Kerala. Unable to face the wrath of trade unions and environmental groups, scores of industrial units in the state had been forced to pull down their shutters in the past.

Kerala gets the highest rainfall in the country. It receives two monsoons – summer and winter – every year. No other Indian state is so lucky with rains. But, the state's environmental groups would rather allow the rainwater to flow down into the sea rather than use it to generate hydroelectric power as that could destroy rainforests, flora and fauna. Some 30 years ago, the government planned to set up a giant hydroelectric power project that would harness this heavy flow of rainwater. Popularly known as the 'Silent Valley Project', it was meant to export electricity to neighbouring power and water-starved states like Tamil Nadu and Karnataka. But it never saw the light of the day in the face of strong resistance from environmental groups and their persistent legal action. If Coke had done its homework well, it would have avoided Plachimada.

It was a huge mistake: Coke soon found itself locked in a bitter battle with Plachimada's 'water warriors'. The recriminations flew between the village Panchayat (a local self-government), a symbol of India's grass root democracy and Coke, and threw up several basic questions. Firstly, what was the social and economic utility of water guzzlers like Coke in a country precariously short of freshwater resources? Next, should there be a strong regulatory framework to discipline water-based non-essential industries like soft drinks and monitor their menacing operations in water-starved locations? Should India encourage companies like Coke to indulge in reckless commercial exploitation of groundwater, depriving millions of people of their right to clean drinking water? India faces a massive shortage of clean potable water for its people; it is a universal problem faced by mega-cities like Delhi, Mumbai and Chennai as well as several hundreds of thousands of villages like Kerala's Plachimada.

There have been several geophysical studies on the earth's proven reserves of freshwater. Coke's own study of global 'water situation' says that 'by 2025, two-thirds of humanity is likely to suffer from a moderate to severe shortage of water'. It says that in India, the per capita water availability is only 1,967 cubic metres as against 10,230 cubic metres in the USA. The 'stress factor' applies when the per capita water supplies drop below 1,700 cubic metres. With 2.45 per cent of the earth's land mass and over 17 per cent of its population, India accounts for only 4 per cent of the earth's freshwater resources. By 2025, the freshwater availability in India per head will fall to 1,600 cubic metres.

In such circumstances, it may be interesting to assess the future of water guzzling companies like Coke and how they can avoid compounding the misery of the country's teeming millions, who are thirsty and unclean for want of water. How many people consume soft drinks in India? According to the industry, it is close to 200 million or less than 20 per cent of its total population. A production of 550 million cases of carbonated water by Coke and Pepsi in 2004 would mean the production of over 3,000 million litres of soft drinks. Going by Coke's claim that it consumes 4 litres of water to make 1 litre of soft drinks, this means that the two soft drinks makers would have consumed 12,000 million litres of freshwater during 2004. Coke's soft drinks business grew at a phenomenal rate of 27 per cent in 2002. Inclusive of its bottled drinking water, the business growth that year was nearly 40 per cent. Despite the pesticides controversy, Coke's volume growth in 2003 was claimed to be 22 per cent. The bottled water business is fast catching up with the soft drinks business in India. The size of the bottled water business (retail packs) in 2001 was estimated at 185 million unit cases or 1,052 million litres. This business is growing at an exponential rate of 40 to 50 per cent a year. The introduction of highly popular bulk packs of bottled water, each containing 20 to 25 litres, for in-home as well as institutional consumption will further boost the business in the coming years. It is no wonder that Coke's India operations have come under increasing attack from local communities, especially around its plants that have been accused of exploiting millions of litres of groundwater every day and fouling the environment as well.

The pygmies of Plachimada have been fighting corporate goliath Coke since 2001 because of over-exploitation of groundwater. The Rs 80-crore Coke plant has three production lines – a 600 bottles per minute

(BPM) returnable glass bottle (RGB) line for CSD, a 65 BPM PET line, also for CSD, and 160 BPM RGB line for the juice based drink Maaza. The plant produces all the top brands of Coca-Cola including Thums Up, Limca, Fanta, Sprite and Kinley Soda. The plant's built-up area is 37,103 sq. m. Local and international NGOs working in Kerala say that the Coke plant consumes 1.5 million litres of water per day, extracted mostly from the underground water resources through high powered electric pumps connected with borewells. Coke, however, claims that the figure is exaggerated. Its water requirement varies from 620,000 litres per day during the March–June peak season to 460,000 litres per day for the remaining eight months. Whatever the correct figure, the fact is that the Coke plant consumes a huge amount of water every day in a water-starved area. While the local tribal families, NGOs, newspapers, including *Mathrubhumi, Deshabhimani* and *Kerala Kaumudi,* blame Coke for the falling underground water levels and growing water scarcity in the region, Coke blames the rain god for the water shortage. Coke has also been accused of changing the environment in the region affecting the yield of coconuts, the second most important source of livelihood after paddy for the local people, and 'poisoning' farmland with its industrial waste called sludge. The local Perumatty Panchayat cancelled the plant's operational licence twice on the charges of groundwater depletion, changing the environment and fouling the farmland with sludge generated from the plant. Coke moved the High Court of Kerala, the highest court of judicature in the state on both occasions for cancellation of these orders. However, the court was not inclined to buy Coke's argument and take a decision that would go against the public opinion and strong local sentiments. The company was given temporary relief against the Panchayat action by way of conditional advertisement interim injunctions against the orders of the local self-government.

It is not clear what really sparked the bitter battle between Coke and the local social activists. According to one version, it started with some local tribal leaders seeking some compensation for poor farm workers who lost their jobs after Coke acquired nearly 40 acres of land at Plachimada (Moolathara village) on the Palakkad–Pollachi road. The state of Tamil Nadu, Coke's second largest market in south India after Andhra Pradesh, is only 5 km from the company's Plachimada plant. The rumour was that Coke paid a 'heavy' amount, much higher than the prevailing local market price, to acquire this 'priceless' property. This led to the eviction of several dozen landless tribal workers who eked out a living from the land by working as farmhands on a daily wage basis. Aware of the company's 'deep pockets', the Leftist tribal leaders wanted Coke to compensate their supporters for the loss of their livelihood. Coke rejected the demand, assuming that the small group of landless tribal men and women, poor and famished, would not be able to sustain their agitation for long. It reckoned they would lose patience and look for a livelihood elsewhere. Coke even engaged a few of these tribal men and women as unskilled workers at the plant. But they left after a while to join their people who formed a picket outside the plant. The group did not succumb to Coke's efforts to break their affiliation. On the contrary, they organized a relay sit-in outside the Coke factory to protest against 'over-exploitation' of groundwater by the company, contending that this had led to heavy water scarcity in the village and surrounding areas.

As the peaceful demonstration outside the Coke factory continued for months, this group's fight against the mighty MNC attracted the attention of a lot of people in the district and earned the demonstrators a lot of respect from social and political activists from the other parts of the state. The area was affected by scanty rainfall in 2001 and 2002, exacerbating the severe hardship that the tribal families faced. The drought meant a prolonged heatwave and high demand for soft drinks. The Coke plant operated at full capacity, guzzling millions of gallons of water. In the summer season, Coke also purchased water from outside through contractors, thus tapping water resources in the adjoining areas. Its sludge became an issue after local farmers, who were given this sludge free of cost as rich 'manure' for application on their land, started complaining about its toxicity. The issue was taken up by NGOs. It became the subject of a huge controversy after the visit of a British Broadcasting Corporation (BBC) correspondent who had the samples tested in a UK-based University of Exeter laboratory and found it to be a contaminant. The local people, an NGO and M P Veerendra Kumar, the editor-in-chief of *Mathrubhumi*, one of Kerala's two most influential morning dailies, took up the issue with the JPC which was investigating the pesticides in colas controversy. The JPC's terms of reference did not include such matters as the water consumed by soft drink makers like Coke and Pepsi, or whether the two MNCs paid for the groundwater they used for manufacturing the products, or what Coke did with its 'toxic' industrial sludge. But the JPC Chairman Sharad Pawar decided to look into these new issues after he received a letter from Veerendra Kumar. Pawar even accepted Veerendra Kumar's invitation to visit Plachimada and set a date for the visit which, however, did not materialize because of the Union government's decision to summon an early Lok Sabha session to pass a midterm budget before the national elections.

The charges levelled against Coke before the JPC were specific. While Pepsi's name was also mentioned as the company operated a bottling plant in a more weather-friendly area in the Palakkad district, 10 km away from the Coke unit, Coca-Cola was painted as the main 'culprit'. The BBC's investigative story, broadcast in July 2003, ensured this. The BBC report said in no uncertain terms that the industrial waste provided to Indian farmers by the Coke plant in Kerala contained toxic chemicals. It quoted Professsor David Santillo, a senior scientist of a British laboratory that tested the sludge, as saying: 'What is particularly disturbing is that the contamination has spread to the water supply – with levels of lead in a nearby well at levels well above those set by the World Health Organisation'.

According to a memorandum submitted by a local NGO, which the JPC took cognisance of, 'agricultural operations have also been affected due to the operations of Coca-Cola company within a short span of three years. The working of the HCCBPL factory at Plachimada has brought untold misery to the people in the surrounding villages. After the Cola plant started production, the water levels in the open wells in the area were affected. When protests arose, the Cola company is said to have let into the earth waste water through shallow tubewells. This mixed with surface water, led to the rise of water levels in the wells. However, these waters proved to be contaminated. The operation of the Coca-Cola plant in Plachimada has led to various environmental problems:

pollution of water, groundwater depletion, reduced crop yields and skin disorders and other physical ailments among the inhabitants. The factory is releasing waste water to the tune of 1.5 to 3 lakh litres per day.

The licence to the company was given by the Perumatti Panchayat under certain conditions. As per the laws, the company has to first get a land use certificate for industrial purpose which was not done. It applied for installation of one pump but started drawing water through borewells without prior sanction and began indiscriminate use of groundwater. The District Medical Officer who stipulated certain conditions like protection of public health needs and observation of factory laws, had also instructed that before commencing production there should be a final fitness certificate obtained. But the Cola company did not abide by these'.

On failing to conform to the terms set by the Panchayat when it asked for details, its licence was cancelled. 'The company disputed the very powers of the Panchayat and resorted to the path of litigation than observing the laws and the conditions on the basis of which the licence was issued. On 3 November 2003, the Perumatti Panchayat sought information on various matters relating to the functioning of the plant and violations by the company. HCCBPL, in its reply failed to provide the details sought by the Panchayat and instead asked the Panchayat to reply to their questions'. Coke rebutted allegations over groundwater levels and quality before the JPC. It said: 'The Coca-Cola plant at Palakkad, Kerala, not only complies with all local regulatory requirements, but also adheres to the stringent global company standards. It is certified to Environment Management Systems ISO 14001 and independent studies from Government agencies concerned with the environment have given our plant a clean bill of health [...] In view of the concerns of local people we have commissioned studies into our impact on the water supply and the State Government has also conducted their own tests. Reports from Kerala State Ground Water Board, Central Ground Water Board and an eminent scientist from National Geophysical Research Institute in Hyderabad have, in the last year [2002], confirmed that the plant's operation is not impacting the water supply to the local villages or depleting the aquifer'. Further, the company said: 'We are recharging the groundwater in our Palghat [Palakkad] plant to the extent of 50 per cent'.

Was Coke hiding the truth? The joint sampling of the Coke sludge conducted by both the Kerala State Pollution Control Board (KSPCB) and the CPCB at the Coca-Cola factory itself on 12 September 2003 nailed the lie. The report said: 'Sludge analysis revealed cadmium content up to 338.8 mg/kg. The CPCB has therefore advised the State Board to direct the Company to dispose of the effluent treatment sludge as per the Hazardous Wastes Rules. More detailed study will be done under different production scenario in future. Samples of raw water from individual wells of and around the factories need to be analysed. Samples of raw materials like sugar, lime, soda ash, ferrous sulphate and activated carbon and the intake water need also be analysed. Action in this regard is being taken. In compliance with the Board's instruction, the Coca Cola Company has applied for authorization under the Hazardous Waste Rules. The application is under processing'. In a wider context, the CPCB said, 'they had tested the samples of raw water as well as treated water from different bottling plants in the country and found high levels of cadmium and heavy metals in the sludge from the effluent treatment plants of some of the units'.

Unfortunately, reports by these regulatory authorities are not always trustworthy. They suffer from inconsistency and, it is alleged, they can even be manipulated by industry. The latter takes advantage of such a situation. A senior official of the Kerala government was publicly heckled for giving Coke a 'clean chit' after one such test as some scientists sang a different tune. Some lowly paid government officials and corrupt politicians are known to thrive on corporate scams. The cadmium content in the Coke sludge in Kerala had created a lot of confusion because of the contradictory test reports from the KSPCB. Coke took advantage of this by highlighting the report that said its industrial waste contained no toxins while remaining silent on other reports, including the joint sampling report by the central and state pollution control bodies, which found the sludge hazardous.

A day after the 'pesticides in colas' controversy hit media headlines all over the country, the KSPCB found 'dangerous level' of cadmium, a cancer causing metallic chemical, in the sludge supplied as fertilizer by the Coke plant to farmers in Plachimada, Palakkad. The Board released its test report of the Coke sludge to the media on 6 August 2003 even as a team of experts from the company's global office in America and an independent Coke engaged sampler from the UK was in Kerala to take stock of the situation. The Kerala government's report confirmed the BBC Radio report. The KSPCB Chairman Paul Thachil said Coke was asked to immediately stop the distribution of its sludge and that it would conduct a detailed study on the subject and recommend further action against the company. Thachil said that the permissible limit of cadmium was 50 mg/kg;

201.8 mg of cadmium was present in the Coca-Cola sludge – four times more than the limit. '[...] the sludge may have to be classified as hazardous waste. The Board has therefore instructed the company not to let the sludge out of the factory premises', not to let anyone use it as manure, even within the premises'. Ironically, the same government body had cleared Coke of the charge that its sludge contained toxic contaminants in January 2003, just six months before the independent test report from the Exeter University laboratory in the UK. The state body's report in January 2003 said the cola plant was well within tolerance limits prescribed for waste water treatment, emission of gases and utilization and disposal of solid wastes. Coke held a press conference at Thiruvananthapuram, Kerala's capital city, on 31 July, where the head of the India Division's technical function flaunted the KSPCB January report to debunk the BBC Radio report and the scientific test results of the Exeter University laboratory.

At a charged press conference, Coke's India Division technical head, who had bored media persons with a long-winded PowerPoint presentation showing technical data and reports, stoutly denied that the sludge contained toxins above the permissible levels or that it distributed the waste as fertilizer to local farmers. One can use it as a good 'soil conditioner'. 'We use it ourselves in our factory garden', he said, ignoring the fact that the company had earlier told BBC Radio in a recorded interview that the sludge was passed on as 'fertilizer' to local farmers.

On 5 October 2003, merely 60 days after it blackballed Coke's Plachimada plant with a test report that showed its sludge contained dangerous levels of cadmium, the state KSPCB did a somersault. This time it came out with a test report that gave Coke a 'clean chit' by saying that the average cadmium content in the sludge was only 34 mg/kg. The earlier report had estimated it at 201 mg/kg. For reasons that were never quite explained to the public, the board 'cautioned' the company 'against the use of the sludge as manure'. It was unthinkable that in such a short period of time the cadmium content in the sludge would fall so dramatically. The board's press statement said: 'The wells located around the company and land applied with the sludge as manure are not contaminated with heavy metals like cadmium, lead, chromium etc'. The concentration of cadmium and other heavy metals in the sludge was found to be below the limit under the hazardous waste management rules. The report even kowtowed to Coke, by substituting the word 'sludge' with 'solid waste' in all its official communications on the subject, apparently to provide some respectability to the industrial waste generated by the cola giant. It said: 'The solid waste generated from the company will not come under the purview of hazardous waste. However, the solid waste [...] is not advisable for application on land as manure. Hence, as utmost precaution, the company should handle the solid waste as per the procedures and safeguards prescribed under the Hazardous Waste (Management and Handling) Amendment Rules, 2003.'

The report was self-contradictory; in an earlier sentence it was stated that 'the sludge was found below the limit under the hazardous waste management rules'. If this is true, then why should sludge be treated as a hazardous waste. An extremely jubilant Coke told everyone who cared to listen: 'Didn't we tell you that we are clean, we are safe, we are world class?' The official statement said: 'The Coca-Cola plant in Kerala is a unit that is ISO 14001 certified. We are confident of both our product quality and manufacturing practices. The latest government endorsement will further help strengthen our relationship with local communities'. Coke went gaga over the latest pollution board certificate. It took out scores of copies of the report and circulated it among lawmakers, bureaucrats, politicians, environmentalists, its own employees and media persons. It was a pity that Coke's new-found 'confidence' was doubly dented after the JPC report cast aspersions on both its quality and manufacturing practices. The 'local communities' were soon hell-bent on creating more trouble for Coke. The public heckled the official even before the joint sampling report once again confirmed that the sludge was 'hazardous' with a cadmium content exceeding 50 mg/kg.

It would be unfair to accuse only KSPCB of producing confusing results. The dockets prepared by Coke on its Kerala operations for external consumption, including JPC, were equally confusing, especially if a comparison is drawn between the one prepared in October and the one in November 2003. For instance, the October docket on groundwater levels and quality mentioned the Pollution Control Board's (PCB's) consent to use up to 560 cubic metres per day and the plant's installed capacity at 450 cubic metres per day. The November docket makes no mention of these numbers. In October, Coke put its average daily usage at 400 cubic metres. In November, the number was amended to read as 500 cubic metres. In October, Coke claimed the net average daily extraction of water from the aquifer was reduced to about 100 cubic metres, showing a 75 per cent saving (25 per cent from efficient manufacture and 50 per cent from rainwater harvesting). This was not mentioned at all in the November docket, which some new entries on the subject saying 'extensive water recovery schemes have enabled (Coke) to reduce source water requirement by 240 cubic metres a day and an estimated 45,000 cubic metres of rainwater was recharged between July 2002 and June 2003'. This amounted to 24 per cent of (the plant's) daily water requirement. The October document said that the unit's consumption was only 400 cubic metres a day with about 50 per cent of the water being replenished by rainwater harvesting and recycling. Coke chose to keep this information out of its November document. The October docket carried the Central Ground Water Authority Report of 14 September 2004. The November one replaced it with the Central Ground Water Board Report of 24 September 2003. Also, it did not mention the Kerala State Ground Water Board Report of 9 November 2002, which figured in the October document. The most interesting changes that took place in the two successive documents were with regard to water usage between June 2002 and June 2003. The October document said that the saving in the production process was 100 cubic metres per day and savings of 200 cubic metres per day through rainwater harvesting. In November, it said water usage was reduced to 240 cubic metres per day of source water requirement through more efficient manufacturing and estimated recharge of 120 cubic metres per day through rainwater harvesting. In October, the rainfall prediction for 2003 was 1,500 mm, which went up to 1,700 mm in November. Interestingly, in a document titled 'Facts about the Coca-Cola operations at Palakkad, Kerala', prepared and distributed in September 2003 the company estimated rainfall at 560 mm up to June and predicted that it would go up to 1,100 mm for the whole year. There were more glaring discrepancies in the figures put out in these documents. For instance how many workers were on the permanent rolls of the Coke plant at Plachimada: 140, 180 or 250? How many indirect beneficiaries did the Coke plant have: 5,000 or 7,000? The jugglery with figures was mind-boggling! There was so much of tinkering with facts, data and statistics with regard to Coke's operations at Kerala that even the company might find it tough to trust itself on the actual position. All this for the defence of an indefensible investment decision to set up a water plant in a rain shadow location in an ecologically hyper-sensitive state like Kerala, with a history of industrial strife, Leftist movement and a strong anti-MNC, anti-US sentiment! Coke's public relations exercise harped on an unsubstantiated claim that the 'local people' were supporting the operation. Did the Panchayat comprise of the representatives of local people or of outsiders? Coke said that the waste water was treated as per their specifications. Purified water was used for irrigation within the factory. The factory did not discharge any kind of water outside its premises. There was no environment harassment.

Coke was in no mood to surrender to public demand. Probably, it could not. The stakes were too high for Coke and its business future in India. The only face-saving solution would be to have the company thrown out of the state by its government and the judiciary. In that case, it would at least win public sympathy from other parts of India, and Kerala would once again be damned as 'an investors' graveyard' by the media and the public. But even such a situation would not guarantee a trouble free existence for Coke in India in its present form. Coke already faces water and environment related problems in other states. The developments in Kerala had emboldened the anti-Coke agitations in those states, supported by influential national and international NGOs and organizations like the World Social Forum (WSF) and the People's World Water Forum. A wrong investment decision and a mindless confrontation with the local administration (Panchayat), media and the community to subvert an increasingly popular people's movement had left the world's largest brand with few options. In order to persist with its strategy, Coke employed an Indian PR agency at first for Kerala and soon for various other parts of the country for a huge annual fee plus other costs, believed to be the highest corporate PR billing by any firm in India. The mandate is practically open-ended – from organizing counter public offensive, holding demonstrations, influencing professional and scientific bodies, holding seminars to remove 'misconceptions' about the ill-effects of soft drinks, generating or organizing letters to media editors, ministers, parliamentarians, regulatory authorities, etc. to the routine distribution of press handouts and plantation of stories. In other words, the agency's job is to manage the hostile external environment for the company. The danger of employing such a strategy in a highly complex and pluralistic society like India is that it could boomerang and, in due course, push Coke into deeper trouble. Coke cannot ignore the means it adopts in a water-starved country like India to justify its business objectives and the desire to keep its American shareholders happy.

Coke does not even pay for the millions of litres of groundwater drawn by its plants and those operated by its franchisee bottlers and a large number of contract packers to run its operations. The company merely pays some very small amounts to the government as registration fee for borewells in certain locations. For instance, out of some 29 Coke plants listed in the JPC report, which applied for registration with the Central Ground Water Authority along with the registration fee paid, only six units belong to HCCB and the remaining 23 plants are franchisee-owned. What is the status of the other 21 HCCB owned plants? Do these plants also pay registration fees for their borewells to some regulatory authority or the other? Of the six HCCB plants mentioned, only four are required to pay. The total amount paid for registering 20 borewells at the four plant locations is only Rs 20,500, or equivalent to a day's salary of some of the India Division's senior employees. The name of Coke's Plachimada plant in Kerala does not even feature in the list. Interestingly, this point was not even raised by the Perumatti Panchayat while cancelling the HCCB plant licence with effect from 1 April 2003, which was temporarily stayed by the Kerala High Court. The dispute between the company and the Panchayat was referred to the local self-government for an order after hearing both the parties.

Why did the Panchayat cancel the HCCB licence after renewing it for two consecutive years? The Panchayat gave two key reasons. They were: (i) The water level in the nearby wells had gone down due to the overexploitation of groundwater by the company from the borewells in its compound; and (ii) as a result of the overexploitation of groundwater, the quality of water in the nearby wells deteriorated. It might be interesting to note that at this point of time, the dumping of the plant's industrial waste as fertilizer on local farmers had not turned into a major issue although it was mentioned by the Panchayat's counsel before the court and the government. This could be because of the 'quality certificate' that the KSPCB had given to the plant waste. It became a big issue only after the BBC

Radio's discovery. The counsel for the Panchayat said that 'if the company is allowed to extract the groundwater at this rate, it will lead to drought in the area, putting the people in difficulties [...] Studies conducted by independent agencies revealed that the solid waste discharged from the company contain toxic elements like cadmium and black lead. This indicates that the soft drinks produced by the company contain elements causing serious health problems to the people who drink it. As the Panchayat cannot ignore the interest of the people at large, it cannot but take a decision to cancel the licence issued to the company. Also, the company has violated the Kerala Land Utilization Order in converting the paddy field to construct its buildings. The company has set up more motors than shown in the sketch submitted for the licence. The Panchayat has no objection to conducting scientific investigation to prove the allegation against the company'. The Panchayat counsel's argument did not give an impression that the local administration was after Coke's blood. The Panchayat was concerned about a severe water scarcity in the area under its jurisdiction and, felt Coke's overexploitation of groundwater might have something to do with it. The rural civic body was concerned about the quality of Coke products because of the toxic elements in the solid waste discharged by the company. It had no objection to a scientific investigation to verify the merits of these allegations.

What did the Coke counsel say while trying to set the courts to question the Panchayat's order cancelling Coke's licence? The gist the Coke counsel's argument was: 'The Panchayat has no case. The company has not violated any of the conditions stipulated in the licence issued by the Panchayat. The latter has not obtained any report either from the KSPCB or from the Central

Ground Water Department or from any competent authority to come to the conclusion that the over exploitation of water by the company has resulted in the depletion of water in the nearby wells and the deterioration of the quality of water in some of the wells in the vicinity. Though the report from the water analyst section of the Medical Laboratories, Kozhikode, refers to the degradation of water in some of the wells in the vicinity, it could not be confirmed that it is due to the over exploitation of water by the company from the bore wells in its compound. Similarly, there is no evidence to suggest that the depletion of the water level in the nearby wells is due to the activities of the company. The Panchayat was influenced by extraneous issues like the agitation carried out by some interested groups in the area. The Panchayat has not based its decision on any independent scientific investigation conducted by competent authorities. Also, the Panchayat cannot adduce any fresh evidence to support the decision already taken. The Supreme Court has said that when a statutory functionary makes an order based on certain grounds, its validity must be judged by the reasons so mentioned and cannot be supplemented by any fresh reasons in the shape of an affidavit or additional evidence. The contention of the Panchayat that the studies conducted by certain agencies proved that the solid waste discharged from the company contains toxic elements beyond tolerable limits, suggesting the presence of toxic elements in the soft drinks produced in the company, have no evidentiary value. The company is ready to cooperate with the Panchayat in conducting any scientific investigation regarding the over exploitation of groundwater, the quality of water in nearby wells, the quality of its products and the toxic elements in the discharged waste'.

After hearing both the sides, the secretary to the Local Self-Government Department, Government of Kerala concluded: 'It is a fact that the Panchayat has not conducted any scientific enquiry or obtained any report from competent agencies before taking the drastic step of cancelling the licence already issued by it. It is an admitted fact the water levels in the nearby wells have gone down, but it is not conclusively proved that this is due to over-extraction of groundwater by the Company. It is also admitted that the quality of water in at least some of the wells in the area got deteriorated, but there is no clinching evidence to prove that this is due to the activities of the Company. Though there is force in the argument of the counsel for the appellant Company that the records produced to prove that the solid waste discharged from the Company contains toxic elements have no evidentiary value, it is a fact that enquiries revealed that the solid waste discharge from the Company contains toxic elements. There is some force in the argument of the Panchayat that this is due to the presence of toxic and injurious elements in the materials used for the manufacture of soft drinks. This indicates the possibility that the soft drinks may contain substances injurious to the health of those who drink it. In short, though there is no conclusive evidence to prove the adverse effects of the activities of the Company on the environment and health of the people in the locality, the records produced and the arguments adduced call for a detailed independent investigation to prove that the quality of soft drinks produced by the Company conforms to approved standards and that the activities of the company have no adverse impact on the environment of the area.

Based on this observation and conclusion, the government ordered that the Perumatty Grama Panchayat will constitute a team of experts from the departments of groundwater and public health and KSPCB to conduct a detailed investigation into the allegations levelled against the Company and its products. The Panchayat will take a decision based on this independent investigation as to whether the licence granted to the Company should be renewed or cancelled. The Panchayat will get the enquiry conducted by these agencies and come to a just and fair conclusion based on this enquiry within three months from the date of receipt of this order. All enquiries and investigations should be conducted with notice to the appellant Company. Till the Panchayat takes a final decision on the cancellation of the licence issued to the Company, the stay granted by the Government on 12 June 2003, against the order of cancellation of licence by the Panchayat will continue in operation'.

A series of developments that followed the local self-government order, including the BBC Radio's investigation, CSE's report on 'pesticides in cola' and the state KSPCB release strengthened the hands of the Panchayat. The public outcry against the operations of Coke's Plachimada factory rose to a crescendo by November 2003. The Coke plant once again faced the prospect of closure following a fresh attempt by the Panchayat. The company, once again, went on an appeal before the High Court. So did the Perumatty Grama Panchayat. While disposing of the application, the court made some very interesting observations which will have a far reaching effect on Coke and similar other companies who mercilessly extract groundwater with little concern for the society and ecology. Referring to an 'authoritative statement' by the Supreme Court, the judgement given by the Kerala High Court on 16 December 2003 said: 'It can be safely concluded that the underground water belong to the public. The state and its instrumentalities should act as trustees of this great wealth. The state has a duty to protect ground water against excessive exploitation and the inaction of the state in this regard will tantamount to infringement of the right to life of the people guaranteed under Article 21 of the Constitution of India. The Apex Court had repeatedly held that the right to clean air and unpolluted water forms part of the right to life under Article 21 of the Constitution. So, even in the absence of any law governing ground water, I am of the view that the Panchayat and the State are bound to protect ground water from excessive exploitation. In other words, the ground water, under the land of the 2nd respondent [Coke], does not belong to it. Normally, every land owner draws a reasonable amount of water, which is necessary for his domestic use and also to meet the agriculture requirements. It is a customary right. But, here 510 kilolitres of water is extracted per day, converted into products and transported away, breaking the natural water cycle. A portion of the rain water is stored as ground water and the balance flows away. The ground water stored in normal circumstance is partially depleted by moderate extraction for domestic and agricultural purposes and also by evaporation through vegetation on the surface. Again, when the rains come, the underground reservoirs called aquifers get recharged and the cycle goes on. If there is artificial interference with the ground water collection by excessive extraction, it is sure to create an ecological imbalance. No great knowledge of science or ecology is necessary to infer this inevitable result. If the 2nd respondent [Coke] is permitted to drain away this much of water, every land owner of the area can also do that and if all of them start extracting huge quantities of ground water, in no time, the entire Panchayat will turn into a desert [...] Therefore, I feel that the extraction of ground water, even at the admitted amounts by the 2nd respondent [Coke] is illegal. It has no legal right to extract this much of national wealth. The Panchayat and the State are bound to prevent it. The duty of the Panchayat can be correlated with its mandatory function No. 3 under the third schedule to the Panchayati Raj Act namely, "Maintenance of traditional drinking water sources" and that of the State to Article 21 of the Constitution of India. Though ground water is not expressly mentioned, Section 218 of the Act makes the Panchayat the custodian of all natural water resources. Therefore, the action by the Panchayat against the 2nd respondent (Coke) to prevent extraction of ground water has to be upheld. So Ext.P6 [executive] order, to the extent it allows the 2nd respondent [Coke] to continue the extraction of water till the Panchayat decides the matter with the help of experts, cannot be sustained. Even assuming the experts opine that the present level of consumption by the 2nd respondent [Coke] is harmless, the same should not be permitted for the following reasons:

1. The underground water belongs to the general public and the 2nd respondent [Coke] has no right to claim a huge share of it and the government have no power to allow a private party to extract such a huge quantity of ground water, which is a property, held in trust.
2. If the 2nd respondent [Coke] is permitted to draw such a huge quantity of ground water, then similar claims of other landowners will also have to be

> allowed. The same will result in drying up of the underground aqua-reservoirs'.

Coke went on another appeal against the order of the single judge before a division bench of the Kerala High Court. Under the order of the Division Bench, an expert committee was appointed on 20 December 2003, to look into the matter and submit a report.

The JPC was also expected to look into the issue although it was not part of its terms of reference. A large number of people of Kerala had approached the JPC and its Chairman Sharad Pawar urging the committee members to get a first hand impression of how the Coke plant had affected the life of the people under the Perumatty Panchayat. The committee chairman agreed. Unfortunately, the promise could not be fulfilled because of an early session of Parliament. However, the JPC report did touch upon the subject on the basis of the allegations by an NGO, Coke's presentation of its side of the story, and other developments including the High Court proceedings.

In conclusion, the JPC report said: 'The other area of concern to the committee is the use of ground water by the soft drink manufacturing companies as well as bottled water manufacturing companies. The committee finds that though these companies are extracting huge amount of ground water, they are not being charged anything for using the water. The only charge that they pay is a petty amount as water cess which is being levied by the State Pollution Control Boards under Water (Prevention & Control of Pollution) Cess Act. States also do not seem to have a uniform procedure in this regard as in some states, industries located in the industrial development areas are charged for the use of ground water at rates decided by the concerned states while in others there is no such practice. Though the Secretary, Ministry of Water Resources, tried to put forth the legal position in this regard before the committee by stating that no charges can be levied on the use of ground water because legally speaking the land and the resources located under it belonged to the owner, who is free to use his assets in the manner he likes, but in view of the recent judgement delivered by the Hon'ble High Court of Kerala on 16.12.2003 in the case of Plachimada plant of Coca Cola India, the stand taken by the secretary loses relevance. The Hon'ble High Court has opined in no uncertain terms that the use of water is free only in case the same is used for domestic or agricultural use by the owner and, since ground water belongs to the public, its commercial use has to be adequately restricted and even in the absence of any law governing ground water, the Panchayat and States are bound to protect ground water from excessive exploitation. The Secretary however had assured the committee that in future perhaps the water if used for commercial and industrial purpose will have to be charged. The Committee, however note with utter dismay that the Central Ground Water Authority (CGWA), which has been constituted as an authority on the direction of the Hon'ble Supreme Court of India, taking into consideration the urgent need for regulating the indiscriminate boring and withdrawal of ground water in the country, has so far hardly taken any concrete steps to properly regulate or coordinate effectively the extraction of ground water for industrial purposes. Taking into account [that fact] that the water level in many parts of the country is getting depleted alarmingly, the Committee desire that this requires to be properly regulated so that at least on account of indiscriminate use of water for commercial purposes, the level does not go down further. The Central Ground Water Authority must take immediate steps in this regard and also impress upon the state governments to do so without further loss of time. The committee notes that water being a State subject, the central legislation cannot be enacted unless the concerned states legislatures pass a resolution and only a few states have enacted laws to regulate over-exploitation of ground water. The committee desires that the Ministry of Water Resources must pursue the matter vigorously with the States and impress upon them the need to regulate water particularly for commercial purposes and also fix the price for water after taking into account the price being charged for water used for domestic purposes'.

The JPC strongly recommended that the water and environment issue involving Coca-Cola and Perumatty Panchayat should be resolved on a scientific and realistic basis. Coca-Cola should take into account 'the strong sentiments of the local people and various environmental issues positively'. The committee wanted the state government to 'intervene in this regard and take necessary steps to resolve this serious issue [...] The Hon'ble Supreme Court of India has constituted recently a monitoring committee on hazardous waste management. One of the terms of reference of this committee serviced by the Ministry of Environment & Forests is to oversee the implementation of hazardous waste management and submit a report to the Court on a quarterly basis. It has jurisdiction over the entire country'.

The JPC suggested that the monitoring committee be engaged to take stock of the 'discharge of effluent sludge in Palakkad and Plachimada' as well. Did the JPC determine whether the problem of hazardous waste disposal was unique to plants at Plachimada and Palakkad? Or, does it exist across the Coke system in the country? If it does, the Supreme Court appointed monitoring committee may remain fully occupied with a single company alone. A reliable and independent assertion of the level of contamination in the industrial waste from the plants, selection of proper landfill sites and strict adherence to the storage and disposal manual are essential if the court and the government are serious about dealing with the issue. It is true that no Coke plant had an issue with the KSPCB until the Plachimada issue snowballed into a crisis. Few will trust Coke after this.

The JPC report on the 'free' use of groundwater by the beverage industry suffers from a lack of in-depth knowledge on the subject. To understand the subject one needs to go deep into the Union Water Resources Department secretary's innocent remarks to find out the truth. The genesis of the problem lies in the industrial policy of the Union and state governments. The policy of industrial dispersal, backward area incentive, lack of primary infrastructure like the availability of water and power for industrial units in the rural areas, shortage of funds with the state governments to undertake large water projects to feed the industry, allowing industrial units on farmland, tribal land and water-scarce areas are among the reasons for the free and reckless exploitation of groundwater by industry. The single biggest culprit is the 'backward area incentive' offered by state governments. Some companies have taken full advantage of this incentive scheme to grab cheap farmland or tribal land and freely exploit all the local resources, including free water and cheap labour, and earn millions of dollars in various tax savings for 'doing a favour to the government and the local people'.

Many companies have taken advantage of this industrial policy to set up highly hazardous industrial units in the backward areas just to distance them from the public gaze and freely pollute the area with their industrial effluents and toxic emissions. This explains why Union Carbide of the US chose an obscure place in the outskirts of Bhopal in industrially backward Madhya Pradesh to set up its most lethal chemical plant. The people and the government came to know about the Union Carbide plant's activity only after an accidental gas leak that caused the world's biggest-ever industrial disaster killing some 10,000 innocent people, mostly the disadvantaged, and crippling many more in the area. Few companies like Tata Steel, the government's own Steel Authority of India Limited and Indian Aluminium have invested substantial funds in creating their own water reservoirs to meet their massive water needs. Other water guzzling industries mostly meet their requirements from municipal supplies, nearby rivers or lakes, or from underground sources. The lure of backward area incentives has induced even respectable large industrial houses to do crazy things.

One of northern India's largest tyre manufacturing plants located in water-starved Rajasthan meets its massive water requirement by transporting water from far flung areas in large tankers. A mere ban on the extraction of groundwater by industry for commercial use or the imposition of cess on groundwater used by industrial units is unlikely to solve the problem of water depletion, especially in water-starved districts or regions. Water has become a big business in many parts of the country. Water contractors are thriving not only in and around cities like

Mumbai, Chennai, Ahmedabad, Bangalore and Delhi, but also in water-starved semi-urban and rural areas. Most of these contractors use private borewells and open wells to fill their tankers practically at no cost. Most of these contractors are local goons and political leaders. They rarely face any opposition from the local community who are afraid to raise a voice of dissent against these powerful water thieves. Their clients include large hotels, restaurants, multi-storeyed buildings, entertainment centres, residential complexes, industrial units, including PepsiCo and Coke. Out of 15 units that manufacture Pepsi products in India and claim to pay water charges, only four depend entirely on their own borewells and tube wells. The rest of the Pepsi plants depend heavily or entirely on supplies from local contractors or government and municipal agencies. Soft drinks manufacturers make maximum use of their borewells during the summer months, the peak season of their business and the worst season for the common man in terms of water availability.

A look at the locations of some 70-odd Coke plants in India, including the company's contract packers, will show that nearly all of them are situated in semi-urban peripheral areas and rural locations using underground water, mostly free of cost. In contrast, rival Pepsi has been more careful about its source water; 40 per cent of the Pepsi's 15 JPC-listed plants are located in notified industrial complexes using the government or municipal supplies and another 40 per cent are heavily dependent on water contractors. This explains why Pepsi's operations attract hardly any public criticism and protests. The sheer greed of making millions of dollars in incentives seems to be the only plausible reason behind Coke's strategy to set up plants in remote backward areas and tribal districts.

Coke also uses water contractors. Of course, water from contractors' tankers does not come free. The underground water within the plant premises does. Commercial considerations also seem to have partly blinded Coke's ethical judgement as the company operated large-capacity units in water-starved regions and states like Karnataka and Tamil Nadu in the south, Maharashtra and Gujarat in the west, Rajasthan and Uttar Pradesh in the north and Madhya Pradesh in Central India. Coke's plants at Wada (Maharashtra), Shiva Gangai (Tamil Nadu), Ahmedabad (Gujarat), Mehandigunj (Uttar Pradesh), Jaipur (Rajasthan) and Bhopal (Madhya Pradesh) are potential Plachimadas.

The Shiva Ganga plant has been ready since late 2002, but it is unable to go into production because of the objection by the local public on the ground that the area is drought prone. The government also has been hesitant to accord clearance to the project in the face of strong public sentiment and overall water scarcity in the region. To win over Tamil Nadu's then Chief Minister J Jayalalitha, Coke's group president from Hong Kong met her along with senior officials of the India Division. The Group President Patrick Stewart promised to help minimize the perennial water shortage problem at Chennai by offering to work with the state government to set up a large sea water desalination plant. This appeared to be one of those 'feel good' promises big bosses of large industrial corporations are known to make in developing countries. Few such promises really materialize. Corporations are not charitable organizations. There is no free lunch. The Tamil Nadu chief minister did not appear to have been impressed. The massive investment in the Shiva Ganga Project continued to remain dead despite the best efforts by Coke and the highly influential franchisee promoter of the project.

Like its Plachimada plant, the Wada unit, also situated in a remote tribal area, was threatened with closure by the Thane district authorities and the local minister, following massive protests against overexploitation of groundwater by the plant in 2003. The Shiv Sena, a militant opposition party, raised the Wada plant issue in the Maharashtra Legislative Assembly. Billed as the largest beverage plant in the Coke system in the whole of South Asia, the Wada unit has as many as 12 borewells inside the factory – all connected with high-powered electric pumps to suck up and lift huge quantities of underground water within hours. Coke had secured permission from the state's Irrigation Department to draw water directly from a river, Vaitarana, situated about 12 km away from the plant. The company had laid a pipeline and set up a small pumping station to lift the water from the river and take it up to the plant. The river, which also serves as a lifeline to the villagers dwelling along its side, gets enough water only when it is released from a dam built on the upper ridge of the Vaitarana. The Vaitarana dam and its huge reservoir have been the main supply source of fresh drinking water for the Mumbai Municipal Corporation since the British rule. Due to the shortage of water in the Vaitarana reservoir, Coke was asked to suspend its water lifting operation from the lower Vaitarana river. Following the Irrigation Department's order, Coke started buying large quantities of water from contractors and tapped its own underground resources to meet the huge water demand of its plant. The villagers around the Coke plant blamed the company for the water crisis in the region.

As in the case of Plachimada, Coke set up a water harvesting unit to recharge the underground water during the monsoon. Since the plant is situated in a hilly region, one cannot be too sure about who will be the ultimate beneficiary of water harvesting. Moreover, rainwater can be harvested only if there is enough rain. While the Plachimada plant is located in a rain shadow area, the rainfall trend at Wada is quite erratic. When the company launched a massive PR campaign with the Thane district administration, political parties and the media to prevent the closure of the Wada plant in May 2003, and continued its pro-active dialogue with these external constituents till the middle of June – the rain god ultimately came to the rescue of the company as heavy monsoon rains lashed the region for the next two months. The Vaitarana river had a normal flow of water. Both the plants are located in tribal dominated areas.

The issue of groundwater extraction by Coke's unit near Jaipur in the desert state of Rajasthan was raised in the State Assembly as well. The company's Mehdiganj unit near Varanasi in Uttar Pradesh created a law-and-order situation in the summer of 2003 as the police baton charged irate demonstrators to protect the plant from their wrath. The demonstrators, led by one of the state's most respectable social workers, had been demanding the closure of the plant on the charge of groundwater depletion and the contamination of private farmland with its effluent water. According to a local NGO, Sanjha Sanskriti Manch, the water level in the area had gone down by nearly 40 feet because of the massive extraction of groundwater by Coke. The plant, located in the heart of highly fertile farmland, was rated among the best performing units during the peak summer season of 2003.

This should serve as an indicator of the nature of water extraction by the plant management during this period. The only good news for Coke was that it faced no major problem in West Bengal, where a Marxist government has been in power for over a quarter of a century, despite the presence of a high level of toxin (cadmium) in the sludge generated in at least two Coke plants. There were no local protests or agitation against the Coke plants. West Bengal's PCB was extremely cooperative in working with Coke to deal with the problem. Take China for instance where it has achieved a record growth. But Marxists in opposition can spell trouble for Coke, as in Kerala. Ironically, Coke's Plachimada plant also came up during the Left Democratic Front's rule in the state with special support from its Marxist industry minister. But the Left parties, currently in opposition, have become sworn enemies of Coke in Kerala.

Although Coke's Kerala plant grabbed the lion's share of the media publicity for overexploitation of groundwater and contaminating farmland with toxic sludge, as many as five other wholly-owned Coke plants in the country were accused by the government of generating industrial waste that contained unsafe levels of heavy metals. Fortunately for Coke, these plants did not attract the sort of strong and persistent attack from the local community and NGOs that the Kerala plant did. The CPCB, which tested samples of water as well as sludge from these bottling plants, had sent its report to the JPC. It said that the sludge generated from some of these plants 'were found hazardous as cadmium (Cd) content was found more than 50 mg/kg'. The five plants identified include: HCCBPL, Varanasi (UP), HCCBPL, Thane (Maharashtra), HCCBPL, Dasna, Ghaziabad (UP) and

HCCBPL, Bidadi, Bangalore (Karnataka). Following the CPCB's communication to the JPC on Coke's so-called treated sludge from these plants, the committee made a few interesting enquiries with Coke's India Division. Coke was asked: whether its plants located all over India were required to get an Environment Impact Assessment (EIA) clearance from state or central PCB; if so, what did these reports say; and, if not, on what basis did these plants secure an exemption from EIA. The JPC also asked Coke to explain 'what steps have been taken by your plants to adhere to the international specific standards under the Environment Protection Act'.

At Plachimada, Coke had doggedly defended its groundwater extraction practices and the quality of sludge, saying the plant was an ISO 14001 certified unit and it complied with the global company's highly stringent environment management system, including periodical environment audit. The CPCB, however, found flaws in Coke's operational practices not only at Plachimada but also at a number of other plants in the country operated both by the company and its franchisees. No information is available about the status of the company's large number of contract packers. The reference to these contract packers and their practices was conspicuous by its absence in the JPC report.

With the company's operation facing increasing public criticism in several parts of the country, Coke's response to the charges on over-extraction of water and its contribution to drinking water crisis around its plants, in terms of water availability and quality, has been typical – there is scientific data to prove such allegations; water shortage is due to scanty rainfall; the company's requirement is met substantially (50 per cent at Plachimada) through rainwater harvesting and recharging the groundwater; the company provides employment and creates business opportunities for the local people; other industries are also tapping groundwater and consuming more water per unit of production; and so on. The Plachimada crisis added a new dimension to this communication package. Coke said it was beneficial to the society if the company's 37-acre plant site produced fizzy drinks than, say, paddy. The reason given by Coke is that paddy cultivation on the same plot of land will not only consume more water, but also employ fewer people and achieve an output that will be several times lower than that of Coke. Therefore, it makes sense to produce Coke than use the land for other activities, including growing paddy. It is no wonder that the people of Kerala made fun of Coke with such snide remarks as 'no food, drink Coke' and 'no water, drink Coke'.

Coke had already lost its fight in the people's court. On 8 March 2004, the Kerala government ordered suspension of thc Plachimada plant's operation till 15 June 2004. The government clearly said the villages in the Plachimada area were facing an acute drought and the soft drink company should refrain from using groundwater until 15 June. The south-west monsoon normally hits Kerala around 1 June. Obviously, the government wanted to see how it progressed over the next 15 days before the Coke plant restarted operations. The government order dealt a big financial blow to Coke's operations in the southern region since March and June are the peak months of the soft drinks business. The Plachimada plant serves not only the Kerala market but also a large part of the burgeoning soft drinks market in the neighbouring state, Tamil Nadu. The government order was also seen as a slap on the face of Coke, which had consistently maintained that its operations were not responsible for water depletion in the area. This time, the company could not secure another interim stay order from the court to keep its Plachimada plant in operation to make the best of the summer of 2004. As early as 17 March 2004, Palakkad recorded the day's highest temperature at 40 degree Celsius, the most ideal weather for soft drinks sale. While its appeal against the executive order before the Kerala High Court was still pending, Coke had no choice but to shut down the plant for a short while. The mighty KO of New York's Wall Street was finally kayoed by the little-known Perumatty Panchayat in Kerala. The Coca-Cola Company acquired the short name KO from the New York Stock Exchange. Pepsi is popularly known as PC on Wall Street.

Coke's cup of woes had yet to reach its brim. There was an 'inspired' leak in the local media that the company was looking for a local buyer to get out of Kerala and that it was in talks with one of its business partners, NeST Foods & Beverages, to palm off the problematic Plachimada plant. On the face of it, it appeared to be a sensible move, which Coke denied. But, the news irked the anti-Coke agitators who shifted their focus to NeST, one of Kerala's highly admired enterprises. Coke's contract packer and distributor of 'Kinley' packaged drinking water in Kerala, NeST voluntarily suspended its operations on 18 March 2004. Its water plant near Perumbavoor in Kochi district, one of the state's several rain surplus areas, was shut down even as a local village welfare standing committee passed a resolution recommending the ban on the use of groundwater for manufacturing Kinley under pressure from the local people and accusations that NeST's bottling operation was responsible for depletion of the water table in the area.

The local Vazhakulam Panchayat committee wanted 'an expert panel to look into the allegation of the misuse of ground water' by NeST. The company said its plant was being targeted as part of the 'ongoing vilification campaign' against Coca-Cola in the state. 'Our plant in Manjhapetty (near Perumbavoor) is not located in an area notified by the groundwater authorities. The charge that we are drawing between 1.5 to two lakh litres of water daily is absurd. The fact is that in our three years of operations, Kinley's average daily sales has never crossed 30,000 litres', a NeST official told the financial daily, *The Hindu Business Line.* The trouble is the average daily sales do not give a correct picture of the peak season sales or the summer sales of cola companies. The business is highly seasonal. Summer sales account for 60 to 70 per cent of the annual sales of soft drinks and bottled drinking water in India.

The local pressure groups also accused NeST of supplying tanker loads of water to Coke's Plachimada plant before it was shut down on 9 March. This is the first time that a contract packer or a business partner of an accused company was made to suffer for its commercial association with such a company. The action against NeST will have a wide ramification on the operations of not only Coke, but also its business partners elsewhere in the country as the MNC is increasingly using the 'contract packing' route to expand its business. The business model is designed to cut the investment cost on business expansion and help Coke disassociate itself from the local troubles that its own bottling plants faced. The successful implementation of the time-tested model, employed by most MNCs and large business enterprises in India and other countries, helped Coke expand its business substantially during 2002 and 2003. By attacking NeST, the anti-Coke lobby in Kerala sent a warning to those who actively participated in the company's soda and water business. The hate campaign against Coke in Kerala has generated such deep resentment in the state that the company may never find it easy to do business in the state – with or without the Plachimada plant. So deep is the hatred against the brand Coke in Kerala that its last ditch attempt to refurbish its image by engaging Mammootty, one of Malayalam cinema's top stars, as its brand ambassador in south India, ended in a publicity disaster. Under public pressure, the film star, who is also the chairman of the state's Left-leaning television channel, Kairali, openly declined to accept the Coke offer. 'I have not accepted the brand ambassadorship of Coca-Cola', Mammootty told the media and added that 'I want to make it clear that I haven't taken up the promotional job'. Thanks to Marxist Mammootty's public statement, Coke was seen as a villain trying to indulge in political intrigue that, if successful, could highly embarrass the CPM's state unit and other Left groups. The possible Coke–Mammootty tie-up for the former's brand promotion was interpreted as a coup of sorts. A visibly upset V S Achuthanandan, a staunch Marxist and the leader of the opposition in the State Assembly, spearheading the anti-Coke agitation in Kerala, said the film idol was loved by the masses and he should not do something that would shatter the sentiments of millions of his fans.

Will Coke face in the near future a similar resistance in other states where its operational practices have already become a matter of debate in their respective legislative assemblies? Much will depend on how the company deals with its detractors. Coke must change its operational style and attitude towards its stakeholders. The company must recognize early the sensitivities and concerns of the local people and institutions and win the trust of the people. There are some 20-odd manufacturing plants in the Palakkad district, which use a lot of groundwater. They have no problem with the community. They have no problem with the regulatory authorities. Their plants have been operating smoothly. Unfortunately, it is not easy for a company like Coke where attitude means everything. Its nineteenth century cowboy culture (Coke was set up in 1886) still permeates through the company's management style and practices. Coke may break, but is unlikely to bend. Once the flag bearer of American capitalism, Coke today has more enemies than friends in rich countries in the West. Their contribution to Coke's troubled existence in Plachimada is no less than that of the Perumatty Panchayat.

12

Plachimada Goes Global

The science and technology section of the *Economist* carried an interesting article on conservation under the headline: 'Who guards the guardians?' The story was about an organization called the Elephant Family, 'itself a species of NGO', auditing the efforts of 21 NGOs in ten countries which claimed to be in the business of preserving the Asian elephant. It began by saying, 'Here's a novel idea: auditing NGOs. Non-governmental organisations, as many charities are pompously described these days, often escape the sort of scrutiny that they themselves like to apply to governments and companies. But, NGOs are human organisations, too, with all the scope of laziness, inefficiency and corruption that any group of people risks falling into if it lacks either self-discipline or external scrutiny'. The Elephant Family had commissioned two researchers for an audit of those conservationists who spent US $4 million a year on the job. Their report referred to, among other things, 'competition of funds and publicity among the larger NGOs'. Funds and publicity are basic to the survival of any NGO. Nowhere was this more apparent than in the case of the two-year long NGO trial of Coke's Plachimada unit in Kerala that was conducted through websites and continuous agitation against the plant. It brought the world community of NGOs to the doorstep of the Coca-Cola factory to condemn corporate exploitation of groundwater in Third World countries with particular reference to TCCC. This is not to say that the global campaign itself was for a wrong cause, or that the company did not deserve it. But it was based on highly exaggerated information dished out by some of these NGOs and conservationists either intentionally for big publicity, or because of ignorance and carelessness.

Coke's travails to defend its Plachimada plant against persistent attack from conservationists and social activists began with an NGO claiming that the company was sucking up all the groundwater in a poor tribal village in Kerala, by boring 600 wells, all operated with high powered electric pumps, inside its 37-acre plant. The cause was soon taken up by conservationist Anita Roddick, who is also associated with The Body Shop, one of the world's best known body care brands. No one cared to cross-check with Coke or the village administration to find out how many wells had been bored inside the plant – 600, 60 or only 6? Did the practicability of sinking 600 or even 60 borewells inside a plot of this size ever occur to these NGOs and conservationists? The 37-acre plot also houses a large manufacturing plant with attended facilities inside like roads, loading–unloading bay for finished products and raw materials, storage place for glass and plastic crates, and an administrative office. Does it leave enough space for sinking 60 borewells and two mid-sized open dug wells outside the built-up area and the storage and transportation facility of the plant? Who will question these NGOs? Like several others, Anita Roddick's website did not appear to be particularly concerned about such trivialities. In their crusade against 'capitalist pigs' fouling up the environment for commercial gains, they could afford to lose sight of a few vital numbers or issues as long as they generated enough publicity. Anita Roddick's report was highly effective. The sensational information on the website about Coke's 'ruthless' exploitation of nature and the poor people of Plachimada did the trick. It made the world's largest non-alcoholic beverage company sit up and think how it should handle a possible international media onslaught on its India operations. For the first time since the anti-Coke agitation by the local people began a year ago, the company's Hong Kong-based group office appeared to be nervous. Given Anita Roddick's credibility with the media, public, pressure groups and NGOs, the group office was worried that it was only a matter of time before Coke's Plachimada operations came under the scrutiny of investigative reporters from major international media.

In all fairness to Anita Roddick and other websites, the information on the exploitation of groundwater by the Coke plant in Plachimada and the water crisis in the region had some truth although some details like the number of wells inside the company's Kerala unit were on the higher side. It is also true that these websites overlooked similar operations by other water-based industries in the district of Palakkad, including the PepsiCo plant, giving an impression that they were more interested in gunning for Coke rather than pursuing issues like commercial exploitation of groundwater, contamination of water and disposal of toxic industrial waste. One reason could be that the other water-based industrial units were neither located in rain shadow areas, nor were they engaged in a direct conflict with the local people and their respective village administrations. The lone industrial unit operating within a cluster of tribal villages, all facing severe water shortage was that of Coke. The Coca-Cola unit was entirely dependent on groundwater while most other plants had access to surface water meant for irrigation and industrial use. Anita Roddick's website did the job that Kerala's local NGOs, newspapers and television channels had failed to do for almost a year. The ongoing agitation at Plachimada had not attracted much attention from major national newspapers and television news channels. Thanks to her provocative piece, Plachimada became a global concern. The western media, helped to expose the truth about Coke's operation in the rain shadow tribal village of Plachimada and made the outside world aware of the plight of the local community. The trial by the western media of Coke's functioning in a tiny Indian village was extremely effective. The globalization of a local issue opened the eyes of the state administration, central and regulatory authorities, judiciary and even MPs. Not only was the Plachimada plant forced to shut down, but also its Indian business partner NeST, bottling Kinley water for the MNC, operating a unit in water surplus Kochi met with the same fate following objections from the local community. More painfully for Coke, while its plant at Plachimada had to be shut down in the hot summer of 2004, arch-rival PepsiCo's unit in the same district operated almost normally.

Of all the reports about Coke's 'anti-people, anti-environment' operations in India that appeared in the global media since Anita Roddick's piece, a BBC Radio programme was the most devastating. The latter opened almost a floodgate of enquiries into the MNC's operational practices in India revealing new results and controversies. Among the international media organizations regularly bombarding the company with leading questions demanding instant response were *The Guardian* (UK), *The Independent* (UK), *The Times* (UK), *Financial Times* (UK), *Daily Mirror* (UK), *Le Monde* (France), *New York Times* (US), *Washington Post* (US), *Atlanta Journal-Constitution* (US), *Fortune* (US), *Ashahi Shimbhum* (Japan), *Strait Times* (Singapore), Deutsche Welle (Germany), Australian Radio, Agence France Presse, Associated Press, Bloomberg and Reuters. This was enough to focus the attention of the world on Coke's operations in a tiny Indian village, the miserable condition of the local people and how the latter were fighting back. This was a great human interest story. Coke tried its best to sell its counter point through copious fact sheets and pages of scientific data. The dry, sapless documents read more like statistical records that projected Coke as an arrogant MNC, insensitive to the local community and its genuine concerns. The cocktail of facts were often revised and appeared contradictory. Not unexpectedly, the so-called facts, irrelevant information and lack of uniformity in the statements did not find many takers among experienced media persons. The popular 'Face the Facts' programme on 'BBC Radio 4' on 25 July 2003, featuring Coke's operations in Plachimada, exposed the wide gap between what the company preached regarding protection of local environment and what it practised in the small, once sleepy Kerala village housing its state-of-the-art water plant. Presented by the inimitable John Waite, the 27-minute-long radio programme produced by Susan Mitchell was devastating. It demolished Coke's defence of its Kerala operations including its disposal of industrial waste on local farmland after it heard several villagers, politicians, farmers, scientists, environmentalists and, of course, the company's spokesman.

What did the interviewees say? They blamed Coke for robbing the community of their precious resource, water, by depleting it, and also polluting it. The presenter had some really tricky questions for Coke. Did Coke conduct an EIA of the site before setting up the plant? Was it shared with the local community? Could a copy be spared for the presenter of the BBC Radio programme? If the water shortage in the area was due to poor rainfall in successive years, did Coke reduce the use of groundwater and cut production? Coke did not seem to have the appropriate answers for such questions. How much water does the plant consume? Coke mentioned the average figures for off-season and peak seasons, which were different from what the company mentioned in its subsequent public communications. Is the sludge from the Coke plant toxic? Coke used the usual line of its plant being a 'zero discharge' unit and the farmers were happy to use the sludge as fertilizer. The company later redefined the sludge as bio-solids and its utility was rephrased from fertilizer to manure and, finally, to soil conditioner, before it was branded as hazardous waste in the JPC report.

The BBC Radio programme was an eye-opener even to Plachimada–Perumatty's local community, those poor tribesmen and tribal women who had been agitating against the plant since 2001, local NGOs and social activists. The Sue Mitchell production was so good and pervasive that the real problem at Plachimada appeared to be even more serious than what the local community and administration thought it to be. The transcript of the BBC Radio programme was translated into Malayalam and distributed to all concerned. The English transcript was also made available to many as few heard the direct telecast of the programme in India. So strong was the impact of the BBC Radio coverage of Coke's Kerala operations and its effect on the lives of thousands of people living in the area that the state government instituted a fresh investigation into the chemical composition of the plant's industrial waste or sludge which was given to farmers as fertilizer. Even the JPC took note of the BBC report, a transcript of which was made available to members of the committee. The BBC Radio did another programme on the Coke plant on 2 January 2004 in its 'You and Yours' series. This time, Coke's India Division head himself participated in the programme. He was 'guided' by a group office spokesman from Hong Kong. However, it failed to help improve the situation, which had worsened since the 'Face the Facts' programme, as Coke had nothing new to offer in its defence. If the BBC Radio's 'Face the Facts' was bad enough for Coke's image and reputation in India and in other parts of the world, it's 'You and Yours' programme was even more damaging.

Things at Plachimada were getting messier and messier as anti-Coke agitators found more and more active support from international NGOs and aid agencies like Greenpeace, Action Aid, Christian Aid etc. in their struggle against the American beverage giant. The company described the involvement of global NGOs in the Plachimada stir as a 'WTO agenda' of these international social and environmental activists to stunt India's economic growth. Coke took up the fight against the Perumatty Panchayat, which was hell-bent on scrapping the company's operating licence in the village to court and, in the process, made more enemies among the people and in the administration.

After BBC Radio, it was the turn of *The Guardian.* The popular UK newspaper's environment correspondent Paul Brown accused Coke's Plachimada plant of 'putting thousands of farmers out of work by draining the water that feeds their wells, and poisoning the land with waste sludge that the company dumped on the farmland as fertiliser'. *The Guardian*'s investigative piece said that the huge extraction of groundwater by the Coke plant to meet the demand for its products in the 'company's fastest growing market' in south India was 'causing such damage to the local economy that the village council which granted the company a licence to operate is now demanding the plant's closure'.

The Guardian's report said the company had to send water tankers every morning to the villagers living close to the plant in order to fulfil their basic requirements. The report mentioned the company's denial that the water shortage had anything to do with its daily consumption of 1 million litres of water from the underground aquifer. The report quoted the charity Action Aid as saying that 'the crisis facing the once prosperous farming area is an example of the worst kind of inward investment by multinational companies in developing countries. In its report to the World Trade Organisation's meeting in Cancun, Mexico, in September the charity says this kind of abuse must be controlled [...] Plachimada was a thriving agricultural community until Coca-Cola set up the bottling plant in 1998. Coconut groves and vegetable crops have had to be abandoned because of the lack of water. Action Aid said thousands of people worked on the land' in and around the village, 'but now only 141 workers are employed at the

[Coke] plant' and up to '250 as casual labourers' (the number could be as low as 100 during the long lean period). 'Peaceful sit-in protests' had been going on outside the Coke's water plant. In a hut set up across the road 'a large Coca-Cola bottle [was] kept in a coffin'.

The Independent carried a report on the same day depicting a poignant picture of Plachimada and the painful life of the inhabitants after the Coke plant came to help in the industrialization of Kerala. The report submitted by a three-member team of *The Independent*, comprising Paul Valley, John Clarke and Liz Stuart, after their visit to Kerala, said, 'Three years ago, the little patch of land in the green, picturesque rolling hills of Palakkad in the Indian state of Kerala yielded 50 sacks of rice and 1,500 coconuts a year. It provided work for dozens of labourers. Then Coca-Cola arrived and built a 40-acre bottling plant next door. In his last harvest, Shahul Hameed, the farmer who owns the modest smallholding, could get only five sacks of rice from the land, and 200 coconuts. His irrigation wells have run dry. Meanwhile, the huge factory extracts up to 1.5 million litres of water a day from the deep wells it has drilled into the aquifer to produce Coke, Fanta, Sprite and the drink the locals call, without irony, Thums-Up'.

The Independent's report pointed out that 'the turbid, brackish water which remains at the bottom of the wells [outside the plant] is too high in dissolved salts to be healthy to drink [the point was mentioned in all media reports], cook with or even wash in'. Some claimed the water 'made them ill'. The newspaper report said 'as the summer and the water crisis intensified, the hardship of the local people [was] worsening [and] so [was] the duel between them and the company. For the past 459 days, there has been a daily picket of the factory. There have been street demonstrations and rallies, and spontaneous blackening of Coca-Cola hoardings. More than 300 people have been arrested [...] It is an iconic dispute, a David and Goliath battle between multinational power and some of the world's poorest people. Many of those affected are classed by the Indian government as "primitive tribals". Most of the rest are dalits – "untouchables". Few in power took much notice when they began to complain, six months after the factory opened, of changes in the quantity and quality of well water. So the anger of the local people grew'.

The report also mentioned visibly shaken and angry Shahul Hameed, whose paddy fields 'looked bone-dry', told *The Independent* team: 'My irrigation pump, which I installed with a bank loan in 1980, use to run for 12 hours throughout the night; now it runs dry after 30 minutes. Coke managed to acquire all the lowest lying land in the area and after digging a series of deep wells they took all the water. It is downright theft'. The report said, 'every day 85 lorryloads [of Coke products] leave the [factory] premises, each containing 550 cases of 24 bottles'. The water siphoned off to produce such large quantity of beverages was enough 'to meet the minimum requirements of about 20,000 people. They have not only lost their water but, with the dried-out farms closing, also their jobs. Those worst affected are up to 10,000 landless labourers', the report added.

The Independent's report also included Coke's version from the latter's global headquarters in Atlanta which said: 'We would like to emphasise that, to the best of our knowledge, these allegations made against the plant in Kerala are untrue. In fact, we believe the allegations are politically motivated. The plant concerned has not drained the aquifers and uses only six bore wells. In fact, the local villages receive tankers of free water supplies each day from the plant to supplement their existing water sources'. The company said it 'was establishing an elaborate system of rainwater harvesting'. 'The real culprit', according to Coca-Cola, was a prolonged dry spell in the area as the rainfall was down 'from 1,213 mm in 2000 to 1,147 mm in 2001 and just 670 mm in 2002'. Coke's statement quoted India's National Geophysical Research Institute in Hyderabad as saying: 'There is no field evidence of overexploitation of groundwater reserves in the plant area. All of this [was] disputed'. The UK newspaper report said 'a local human rights and development organisation, VAK, funded by Christian Aid, claims that state meteorological reports show rainfall rose between 2000 and 2001. Another campaign group, CorpWatch India, challenges Coke's claims about rainwater harvesting saying "how much you save through your rainwater harvesting is not the issue; how much additional load you add to the aquifer is"'.

In this context, BBC Radio's pointer on whether the Coke plant cut down its production in keeping with its claim of successive years of decreasing rainfall would appear to be pertinent. Also, CorpWatch sent water samples from nearby wells to the US for testing. 'The resulting report concluded that high levels of dissolved salts were produced by the fast rate of depletion of the aquifer – and that washing in it would cause "severe hardship"'. 'Aid agency campaigners' had been protesting as well. An Action Aid spokesperson was quoted as saying 'This is a shocking situation where it appears that the rights of a big corporation are being put above those of poor communities'. Similarly, Christian Aid, which called for 'binding international regulations' for companies indulging in commercial exploitation of such scarce natural resource like groundwater, said this was 'a classic case of corporate irresponsibility'.

The global media interest in Coke's Plachimada plant grew constantly since December 2002 when another BBC Radio correspondent, James Smith, landed in the Kerala village to do a feature on the plight of the people of Perumatty because of the company's water plant. It gathered momentum in July 2003 after the 'Face the Facts' programme on the BBC Radio 4. International wire service agencies like Agence France Presse, Associated Press, Reuters and Bloomberg kept up a constant watch on the development at Plachimada with Coke fighting the local village council with all its financial and legal muscle. For the fund-starved Perumatty Panchayat, a prolonged legal battle against Coke, the licence fee from which accounted for a major chunk of the village council's annual revenue, could bring disastrous side effects like inability to pay salaries to the regular staff, maintaining overhead costs and continuing with community welfare projects. Coke was ready to field some of the country's most expensive lawyers to overpower the poor panchayat. The international media did not want to miss any part of this unique battle between the two unequals.

The Guardian carried a huge story on 19 December 2003 after a Kerala High Court judge issued a strong order against Coke. Although local newspapers and regional television channels also carried the judge's order in the case, HCCB versus Perumatty panchayat, the news story in *The Guardian*, filed by its environment correspondent Paul Brown, was most emphatic and caught the mood of the people both inside and outside the courtroom. The story came under an equally long and compelling caption. It said: 'Coca-Cola plant must stop drawing water; Indian bottling factory may be forced to close after judge orders ban to protect village's supply'. The report said 'Coca-Cola has been ordered to stop drawing groundwater for a bottling plant which supplies most of southern India after a court found that it was ruining the environment. In a ruling which threatens to close the 16-hectare (40-acre) Coca-Cola plant in Kerala, southern India, the state's High Court ordered the company to close its boreholes and stop drawing groundwater within a month. A thousand local families had been protesting for 608 days claiming the plant is drawing so much of water it is turning their rice paddies into a desert and killing their coconut palms. They [took this] action in defiance of the state government, which supported the company. The court said that if it was to continue work at the bottling plant, the company must find alternative sources of water, but this is a tall order in an area which has suffered two dry years and has gone months without rain'.

Referring to the court ruling, *The Guardian* story said 'the extraction of groundwater at Plachimada village, even up to the limit admitted by the company, was illegal. The company had no right to extract this much natural wealth and the panchayat (local authority) and the government were bound to prevent it. The court found that groundwater was a national resource which belonged to the entire society. "Groundwater under the land of the company does not belong to it", said Justice K Balakrishnan Nair. "Every land owner can draw a 'reasonable' amount of ground water which is necessary for its domestic and agricultural requirements. But here, 510,000 litres [110,000 gallons] of water has extracted per day, converted to products and transported, thus breaking the natural water cycle". [The judge] also pointed out that the supreme court had stated in earlier orders that underground water belonged to the public and the state should act as a trustee for its protection. Judge Nair said the government also had no power to allow a private party to extract such a huge quantity of groundwater, which could result in its drying up'. The story, which was carried with a file picture with the caption 'a schoolgirl takes part in a protest in Bangalore in August urging people to drink natural beverages', linked other developments surrounding the plant's operation and the company. The judge's order found a mention in the JPC report later and made the state government act against the Coca-Cola plant. It sealed the fate of the plant at least till the middle of June 2004.

The aggressive international media coverage of the Plachimada incident was a good enough reason to provoke the WSF, often described as the Third World's answer to the World Economic Forum (WEF), to hold its six-day global convention in Mumbai, India's financial capital, towards the end of January 2004. Almost simultaneously, the World Water Forum, a WSF offshoot, held a three-day conference in India. It's Indian sponsors chose Plachimada as 'the most ideal venue' for the inauguration of the conference. The WSF convention, the new speaking platform of the champions of a new social order and anti-globalization activists, attracted some 100,000 delegates from 132 countries. India had not witnessed anything like this before. Hundreds of NGOs and trade unions of all hues attended the meet. A small two-day programme was also held in Delhi under active association of the Research Foundation for Science, Technology and Ecology, an NGO led by firebrand environmentalist Vandana Shiva. Coca-Cola India had made some elaborate arrangements to place a motley group of Coke sympathisers, consisting of NGOs, scientists and social activists, in these meetings. Most of them were air-lifted from Kerala and put up in one or two-star hotels. The idea was to interrupt Coke bashers in these conventions. The company's operational practices came under attack at all the three conventions.

The World Water Forum conference at Plachimada, which was particularly harsh on Coke, started with Frenchman Jose Bove giving a call for 'resistance movements to launch a worldwide struggle against transnational companies which exploit natural resources like water, by making it a priced commodity to make profit'. Bove, leader of the Confederation Paysanne, the most powerful organization of French farmers, said: 'We have to globalise our struggle to globalise the hope to live. Water belongs to all people. If you do not have water you cannot live and do your agriculture and other activities. So we are asking water trading companies like Coca-Cola, Pepsi Cola, Vivendi and other transnational companies to close down their operations in Plachimada and other parts of India because they exploit the water resources of the native people. The exploitation of water by these companies has deprived the local people of their drinking water. These companies have to quit because they are doing criminal activity by exploiting the lifeblood of the people. So we have every right to ask them to get out of our lives and get out of the country'.

With Jose Bove's belligerent tone directing the mood of the conference, the rest of the speakers fired salvoes one after another in the next two days. Coke was the prime target of all speakers bloating the confidence level of the Perumatty village council president, A Krishnan, who welcomed some 30-odd foreign speakers and participants, 500 delegates from all over India and a few thousand listeners. Parliament member, N N Krishnadas, whose Democratic Youth Federation of India joined hands with the local Muslim groups to lead the 'boycott-Coke' movement during the Iraq war, promised to intensify 'struggle against the water-hijackers' like Coca-Cola and Pepsi. Dr Vandana Shiva branded Coca-Cola as a 'hydro-pirate' of the world.

Dr Maude Barlow, author of *Blue Gold* and chairperson of the Council of Canadian Public Advocacy Organizations, compared Coke with Union Carbide in her keynote address. The US multinational Union Carbide was responsible for the biggest single human tragedy in history in Bhopal and now companies like Coca-Cola were 'play[ing] with the lives of millions' of Indians, she said. Extending her strong support to the cause of the Perumatty village council, Dr Barlow said the people of Canada and other parts of the world, who were engaged in their worldwide fight to protect their drinking water, were supporting the struggle of the people of Plachimada and other parts of India against MNCs such as Coca-Cola and Pepsi Cola.

At the end of the conference, the World Water Forum adopted a 'Plachimada Declaration' that said 'water is the fundamental right of man. It has to be conserved, protected and managed. [It is our] fundamental and inalienable right to water for people all over the world. The Water Policy should be formulated on the basis of this outlook. The Declaration said, the right to conserve, use and manage water should be fully vested with the local community, which was the very basis of "water democracy". Any attempt to reduce or deny this right is a crime. The production and marketing of poisonous products of Coca Cola and Pepsi Cola [...] lead to total destruction and pollution [...] [endangering] the very existence of local communities'.

Four days after the World Water Forum conference, an American delegation from the International Public Health team came to Plachimada after attending the WSF conference in Mumbai and declared that Coke was responsible for dumping high levels of lead and cadmium into the local environment. Later, the four-member team, led by former Ecuador minister for environment Edgar Isch, appealed to the Kerala Chief Minister, A K Anthony, 'not to extend support to Coca-Cola'. The team members, who included a professor of paediatrics, a medical practioner and a health specialist, told media persons at Kochi that the poor health of Plachimada inhabitants was linked to the operations of the Coca-Cola plant. 'No community's water source should be allowed to be robbed and polluted like this by any plant', Edgar Isch said.

Thanks to the persistent western media interest in Plachimada, the World Water Forum meet got several times more coverage than the WSF conference in Mumbai. Ever since, the Kerala government has been under severe pressure from all concerned to act against the Coke unit. Until the end of January 2004, Coca-Cola India received a lot of support from the state's United Democratic Front government, led by the Congress Party, to run its operations in Kerala. This was only natural. First, it is the job of any democratic government to protect business or industrial investments as long as they run lawful operations and are not in conflict with the society. On both the counts, judiciary is the ultimate arbiter. Second, the movement against the Coke plant was led almost entirely by the political opposition of the ruling coalition group in the state. The Perumatty village panchayat was controlled by the elected members from opposition parties, who were in majority. An acceptance of the panchayat's decision to cancel the operating licence of such a high-profile company like Coca-Cola could mean a moral defeat for the ruling political group at the state level. It would strengthen the hands of the opposition, who would demand the resignation of the government on the issue since the government had supported and protected the plant management against anti-Coke agitation for nearly three years. At the same time, it could not ignore the mounting pressure of the local as well as international public opinion against the American multinational for pumping out daily an average 510,000 litres of groundwater, as claimed by the company itself. Coke was increasingly becoming a liability for the Kerala government and the Congress Party in the state, which in any case remained divided because of internal squabbles.

The ruling of a single judge of the Kerala High Court, the State Legislative Committee's censure of Coke's operational practices, the success of the World Water Forum conference, the widely publicized appeal to Kerala Chief Minister A K Anthony, by Edger Isch of the International Public Health Team and never-ending media queries about the reasons behind the government's inaction against the company were causing constant embarrassment to the state administration. The foreign media played a pivotal role in shaping the local public opinion against Coke. Several local newspapers and TV channels, who for nearly two years held a balanced view about the allegation of water depletion by the Coke plant at Plachimada, too turned against the company because of the position taken by the international media on the issue.

Most of the international media persons, who visited Plachimada and interacted with the local community, the village administration, environmentalists and NGOs, also spent hours with local reporters.

The American company's increasing arrogance in dealing with the international media covering the subject further fuelled the anti-Coke sentiments among the journalists. The interviews with Coke officials on BBC Radio bore testimony of such animosity. The casual manner in which the company treated the foreign media, who had spent a lot of time and money to reach this remote Indian village was anything but professional. Coke showed little respect for the concerns of these media professionals. They were given Coke's frequently revised thick fact sheets, running into scores of pages, loaded with information often irrelevant to a media person. Worse still, the company tried to intimidate these foreign correspondents by sending strong rebuttals to their reports to the editorial management of these 'media outlets', electronic and wire service included. The company acquired a new media image – Quarrelsome Coke.

The Coca-Cola management was unconcerned. Rebuttals to media reports were sent by persons holding high offices such as the group president of the company's East and South Asia operations and senior vice president of Coke's Worldwide Public Affairs and Communications. The company's group president, Patrick T Stewart, came down heavily on *Straits Times* of Singapore trashing a story on Coke's India operations that appeared in the newspaper on 29 January 2004. The story, appropriately headlined 'Cola giants in India running low on fizz', was pegged on the World Water Forum (WWF) conference in Kerala. The focus was on Coke and Pepsi's troubled days in India. Understandably, more footage was given to Coke than Pepsi in keeping with the former's share of the trouble. After a few paragraphs, the story had more archival than immediate news value. It even carried an in-built denial in its first paragraph. Rightly, PepsiCo chose to ignore it. Coke, however, refused to digest any of it.

The New Delhi-datelined *Straits Times* story began thus, 'In a globalised world, often it is not nations but multinational corporations which are seen as the exploiters. Such is the reputation, even if untrue, of the two cola giants, Coca-Cola and Pepsi that they find themselves in the firing line in this country, yet again'. It then goes on, 'Last week, nearly 5,000 activists assembled at a remote village in the southern Indian state of Kerala and demanded that Coca-Cola and Pepsi quit India. It is fashionable nowadays to deride such multinationals to draw the attention of the rest of the world, but the people at the three-day World Water Conference that ended last Friday meant business. The conference on the world's dwindling water resources ended with a demand for boycott of Coca-Cola and Pepsi and the slogan "Coke and Pepsi quit India". The Conference was held at Plachimada, a southern Indian village embroiled in a legal dispute with Coca-Cola over groundwater depletion [...] the conference was hinged on anti-cola brigade. "Plachimada is the finest example of exploitation of Indian villages by multinational companies like Coca-Cola", one conference organiser, the National Front for Tribal Self-Rule said in a statement. Coca-Cola has denied accusations of water depletion and filed documents in court to prove its case'.

The story, then, digs into history. It said that it had not been an easy ride for cola companies in India, though their powerful distribution networks had ensured that vends permeate locations where there is no water supply.

While internationally they had signed stars such as Britney Spears to endorse their products, in India top cricketers and Bollywood stars had made mega bucks as brand ambassadors. 'But it has not all been hunky dory. Recently the Centre for Science and Environment (CSE) made public a report that Coke and Pepsi bottled in India contained pesticide levels above the prescribed norms. The CSE said its tests showed 12 colas contained pesticides residues 11 to 70 times higher than the European Union norms. Though the CSE acknowledged that the colas adhered to Indian norms, it argued that the multinational practised "double standards" selling less clean cola in India than in the EU and United States. The Cola giants are now engaged in a major damage control exercise as a Joint Parliamentary Committee looks into the matter', the report went on.

So upset was Coke with the *Straits Times* report that its Hong Kong-based East and South Asia Group president himself sent a rebuttal to the newspaper saying that the article reflected some of the recent allegations against the soft drinks industry in India, and TCCC in particular, but failed to point out the facts of the situation. The rebuttal, carried by the *Straits Times* on 5 February 2004, said: 'The government of India repeatedly declared that our products are absolutely safe and that our production processes comply with regulations and, in many cases, exceed the requirements. These products meet or exceed the standards of the United States and European Union as well. For example, the allegation that the Coca-Cola plant in Kerala is responsible for the depletion of the groundwater has repeatedly been proven to be unfounded. Within 5 km of the plant there are over 300 borewells operating at any one time while our plant uses only three at a time. Regardless of this, it is the only water-based industry – of which there are nearly 30 in the area – to have installed 40 acres of rainwater harvesting technology. This technology actually recharges the groundwater with more water than the plant uses. We have provided this technology to local villages and schools and also provided tankers carrying fresh water – free – to villagers every day. We are in the business of providing a simple moment of refreshment for billions of people worldwide each day. In doing this in India, we have created thousands of jobs, sourced hundreds of millions of dollars' (sic) worth of local ingredients, generated millions of dollars in taxation payments and raised the income of over a million retailers. Moreover, we achieve all this via world-class manufacturing facilities where we use the same quality assurance system that we use everywhere in the world. We welcome any science-based discussion of our products and business but we remain mystified as to the motivation of those who continue to repeat baseless allegations'.

Coke would probably have had second thoughts about sending such an emphatic rebuttal to the *Straits Times* if it knew what was in store for the company for all its quality claims and good operational practices at the Kerala plant as India's JPC found truth in CSE's allegations and advised the company not to ignore the public outcry against its operations at Plachimada. Within weeks of the submission of the JPC report, the Kerala government forced Coke to shut down its Plachimada plant during the summer months. The JPC's science-based report and the Kerala government's action against the Coke plant were covered by the international media. Was Coke planning to send rebuttals to the media across the globe and take Indian Parliament to task for its motives behind the JPC's unfavourable report? Too much noise had been made about Coke's rainwater harvesting technology as if it was out of a NASA laboratory like reverse osmosis for application in Mars in case the scientists discovered water bodies on the red planet. If the Plachimada village of Kerala witnessed a massive decrease in the rainfall between 2001 and 2003, how could the technology 'recharge the groundwater with more water than the plant used?' Coke said it provided 'this technology freely to local villages and schools'. It would have been interesting to know if any village and school in Kerala had actually accepted and used the technology gift from Coke as of 5 February 2004. The knowledge and practice of rainwater harvesting in India are as old as its civilization.

A few days before the *Straits Times* of Singapore published Coke's rebuttal, the world's largest soft drinks company was involved in a spat with Christian Aid, the international NGO and aid agency, over a report in *Financial Times* (FT), London. The FT report under the headline 'Call for laws on multinationals' responsibilities' was published on 21 January 2004. This prompted a rejoinder from Clyde C Tuggle, the Atlanta-based head of TCCC's Worldwide Public Affairs and Communications Department, which FT carried in the edition of 27 January 2004.

Tuggle said the FT's coverage of Christian Aid's report on corporate responsibility relied entirely on that organization's view of the world and it was disappointing as it was a very partial view. Tuggle wrote: 'While we recognise Christian Aid's interest in calling for international companies to be more accountable in areas of corporate responsibility, targeting Coca-Cola and particularly our plant in Kerala, India, is misleading.

'Far from depleting the local water supply as the Christian Aid report suggests, the Coca-Cola plant in Kerala recharges the aquifers with the same amount of water used by the plant. Our plant is one of some 30-water reliant industries in this area of Kerala but the only one to have introduced 40 acres of rainwater-harvesting technology. Once the state authorities have given permission, we aim to recharge up to three times more water than we use and extend our existing programme of freely providing the same technology to adjacent villages and schools. Again, we are the only company to provide free purified water to the community twice a day. While the water issues are unquestionably important, we wish Christian Aid had acknowledged the facts we supplied previously or visited the plant to understand the situation first-hand'.

Three days later, on 30 January 2004, FT's London and US editions carried an even longer rejoinder to Tuggle's letter from the UK-based director of Christian Aid, Daleep Mukarji, rejecting the 'allegations' of Coke's global head of Public Affairs and Communications function that the Christian Aid report was misleading 'and the implication that we have not reported the full facts surrounding its bottling plant in Kerala, India'. The Christian Aid refutation said: 'We first contacted Coca-Cola more than six weeks before the publication date of our report, 'Behind the Mask: The real face of corporate social responsibility', to solicit its comments. This communication followed our field investigation into the depletion of water supply in the villages surrounding the company's plant in Kerala. Coca-Cola had every opportunity to respond right up to the moment the report went to print, and some of its responses are included. Critically, Christian Aid has repeatedly asked to see a copy of the environmental impact assessment done by Coca-Cola before the plant was built. In response, Coca-Cola has provided two different documents, both of which are undated and neither of which provide satisfactory information.

'Christian Aid is also sceptical about the effectiveness of Coca-Cola's rainwater-harvesting scheme. Rainwater can only be harvested when it falls and the company's own argument is that the local water shortage has been caused by lack of rain. The fact remains that some of the region's poorest people who live in the villages close to the Coca-Cola site are still desperately short of water for drinking, washing and cooking. Coca-Cola's efforts to provide them with water are welcome, but the villagers say the company's deliveries are irregular and insufficient. Meanwhile, the High Court in Kerala has ruled that Coca-Cola must stop drawing water from the ground beneath its bottling plant and find an alternative source'.

A comparison of the contents of the two letters written by two senior executives, one from Hong Kong and the other from Atlanta (US), to the two newspaper editors reveals some interesting contradictions. The Coke letter to the *Straits Times* editor said the company's rainwater harvesting technology actually recharged groundwater with more water than the plant used. On the contrary, the company's letter to FT editor said 'the plant in Kerala recharges the aquifers with the same amount of water used by the plant'. Coke's letter to the FT editor claimed that it was 'the only company to provide free purified water to the community twice a day'. In contrast, its letter to the *Straits Times* said the company 'also provided tankers carrying fresh water – free – to villagers every day'. The fact was that the company had two small ponds inside the factory to catch rainwater for the purpose of recharging the aquifer. The system was ready only after the summer monsoon of 2002. A visit to the site will show the low water level in both the ponds. The underground water, even after the high rate of extraction, would appear to be insufficient to run the plant in full capacity in the summer months, when the company taps the water resources outside the plant through the water supply contractors, a fact Coke has never wilfully stated in any of its communications. Inside the Coke plants there were seven borewells and not six. The seventh had already run dry. Coke does not supply 'purified' water twice a day to villagers. Only two tankers of water procured from outside the Coke plant are known to be provided alternatively to two villages. What does Coke mean by its claim of installing '40 acres of rainwater harvesting technology?' Christian Aid's Mukarji was only polite in his remarks that Coke's responses to the aid agency's queries in two different documents were undated and provide unsatisfactory information.

The spat between Coke and Christian Aid had no impact on the *Economist.* The radically conservative international weekly magazine carried a long commentary on the Christian Aid Report. Noting that corporate social responsibility (CSR) is all the rage, the caption of the *Economist* commentary put it rather succinctly: 'Does it, and should it, make any difference to the way firms behave?' Linked with a 2004 Davos WEF theme of good corporate citizenship, it said: 'Lack of compulsion, however, is exactly what is wrong with current approaches to CSR, say many of the NGOs that first put firms on the spot for their supposedly unethical practices. This week Christian Aid, with Davos in mind, published a report claiming to reveal the true face of CSR. The charity is "calling on politicians to take responsibility for the ethical operation of companies rather than surrendering it to those from business peddling fine words and lofty sentiments" […] It regards CSR as a "burgeoning industry […] now seen as a vital tool in promoting and improving the public image of some of the world's largest companies and corporations"'.

'The report features case studies of Shell, British American Tobacco (BAT) and Coca-Cola – all of them, it says, noted for paying lip-service to CSR while "making things worse for the communities in which they work". Shell, says the report, claims to be a good neighbour, but leaves oil spills unattended to. BAT, it says, claims to give farmers training and protective clothes; contract farmers in Kenya and Brazil say otherwise. Coca-Cola promises to use natural resources responsibly. The report accuses an Indian subsidiary of depleting village wells'.

At the height of the Plachimada water crisis, it would appear that the company was becoming quarrelsome in dealing with the media and external stakeholders. The company in its counter-attack spared none of its critics. Scores of copies of 'fact sheets' about Coke's Kerala operations were travelling all over the world. The intention was to convince critics that everything the company was doing in Kerala was right and the local community was wrong. The latter's allegations were mischievous and politically motivated. The company had a running battle with anyone who sympathized with the local community. After the World Water Forum meets in

Delhi and Kerala, Coke sent a series of rebuttals to those eminent international NGOs and speakers whose views were reported in the media. The company even threatened to take on the BBC after its radio programme 'You and Yours' was aired on 2 January 2004. Coke's Hong Kong-based group office issued a 'media and consumer holding statement' which said the company 'worked closely with the BBC during the preparation of their programme but they have chosen largely to ignore the points we have made, the scientific evidence we have provided and the comments made on the record by the President of our operation in India. The programme contained factual inaccuracies, speculation and omissions which, when combined, have presented an erroneous and defamatory view of our operation in Kerala. In our view, the BBC presented a biased, emotional and poorly researched view of the situation in Kerala and did not provide Coca-Cola with an adequate right of reply. It would be inappropriate to comment further on this specific programme as the company is planning to take the matter to the senior management of the BBC as well as the UK regulator, the Office of Communications (Ofcom) for independent analysis and ruling'.

One may say that an unusual situation often demands unusual response. Coke seemed to be going nowhere with its random rebuttals to the media and blanket invitation to all its critics to come and visit Plachimada and see the 'good work' the company was doing. The company decided to send e-mails to a number of internationally known social workers and conservationists, who attacked Coke's operational practices and ruthless extraction of groundwater in the course of their speeches at the WSF and World Water Forum meetings in Delhi, Mumbai and

Kerala, inviting them to visit the Plachimada plant to witness the company's 'endeavour in water conservation inside the plant and [...] community related programmes in the area'. They included Marie Masson, Tony Clarke and Afsar Jafri. But, these people, who spent all their life for the service of the communities would rather trust a community than a company. Neither the local nor the global community appeared to be impressed by Coke's claims and statistical 'fact sheets'. What concerned the communities, the local administration and the judiciary was the human suffering for want of water, deteriorating quality of water and dumping of industrial waste in and around the Plachimada village, from where the Coke plant extracts 620,000 litres of water every day during the peak summer months as per the company's own admission. The people of Plachimada claimed a much higher extraction rate by the company.

The globalization of Plachimada's local issue had put Coke's entire India Division on the mat before the local as well as the international community. If any single factor contributed to this globalization of Plachimada's problem, it was the company's we-are-right, they-are-wrong attitude from the very beginning. Kerala is not like other Indian states. Its 100 per cent literate population is different. The local people are as stubborn as companies like Coke. The water depletion and dirty sludge issues are not unique to Plachimada. Coke had faced such charges in other parts of India. So far, the company's denials of such charges and its community care claims had managed to avert crisis in those other parts of the country. But, the people of Plachimada and Kerala seemed to be adamant about what they saw and believed as true and not the company's claims. Their queries were simple. If the drought at Plachimada was due to scanty rainfall bringing suffering to the people in the area, why was Coke extracting so much groundwater? Did Coke conduct an EIA study before deciding to set up such a huge water plant in the remote tribal village? Where is the full report? Why was Coke dumping its sludge or industrial waste on farmland as fertilizer or manure or soil-conditioner? They wanted straight answers from the company and not roundabout responses carrying copious statistical fact sheets. If these fact sheets failed to impress the international media, NGOs and charities like Christian Aid and Action Aid, how could one blame the poor, water-starved and suffering people of Plachimada for not trusting the company's fact sheets?

Was there anything else Coke could do to defuse the tension built around its operations in Kerala? How could it tackle such websites as www.alternet.org, which continued to dish out such information like 'researchers found that the plant [Plachimada] had drilled 65 bore holes into the ground, siphoning off a million gallons of water a day?' How could Coke acquire the trust of the community after all those claims and counterclaims and the showdown? Coke could still be honest and transparent in its dealings with the panchayat and initiate a peace process by starting a dialogue with the village council outside the court. The company could offer to shut down the unit and seek the help of the government to relocate its water plant to a more suitable place in the state. Coke could form a plant committee that would have a representative of the state groundwater board, PCB and the local panchayat to make its operations totally transparent and accountable to the public. If that failed, the company could leave Kerala bag and baggage. Such an action would help repair the company's tainted image in Kerala. If Coke had no issues with the community, its consumers, suppliers, distributors and regulatory authorities, its negative coverage would automatically disappear from the local as well as global media. The company must recognize the fact that a perpetual engagement in wordy tussle with the community, NGOs and media on any issue is not the way to set an example of good business conduct. Such acts are counterproductive and self-destructive in the long run. It cannot ignore the social accountability part of its business. All these are easier said than done, especially after the management has already positioned to set these national and international NGOs and media against itself. The trouble is that a number of Coke's water plants in India are located in areas affected by water scarcity.

13

Enfant Terrible

If good business conduct is the need of the hour for effectively and honourably managing operations, what steps has Coke's India Division been taking to meet this need? For any business in a new environment, it takes time for the management to settle down even if it has a ready market, acquired a franchisee network and has a formidable brand like Coke. Ideally, in the beginning, Coke should have had a business leader to steer its India operations for a period of at least eight to ten years.

Several MNCs, including GE of the US, and PepsiCo, followed this practice in India as well as in several other countries. Some of these MNCs had a long business association with India before 1992, the year the government initiated the economic reform programme by lifting restrictions on FDI. These MNCs were present in the Indian market as suppliers, technical collaborators, lenders, reinsurers and so on. They set up their own enterprises in India after the government liberalized the FDI rules. Did Coke conduct a proper examination of candidates to select the right person to lead its India operations at the time of its re-entry or even later? Did Coke follow a proper programme to recruit, create, nurture and retain talent for its India operations? Do Coke's external problems in India have anything to do with such attributes as poor quality, questionable integrity and lack of continuity of persons at the helm of the division? These are important human factors that few companies of repute can afford to ignore. Worldwide it has been proved that business growth and business continuity with least interruptions are best ensured under business leaders of high quality who spend long years at the helm.

To remain at the helm of a business, a leader's quality is not judged merely in terms of his company's balance sheet. Personal integrity, honesty, leadership through continuous innovation and long-term vision, and ability to carry the team and retain talent are equally important for a leader to remain for long years at the top. He is a business philosopher as well as an achiever. Take the case of the 118-year-old TCCC itself, one of the world's best known enterprises of the last century. If any two persons are to be identified for their contribution to the low technology, non-essential carbonated soft drinks manufacturing company's phenomenal rise in the twentieth century, they were Robert Woodruff and Roberto Goizueta. Between them, they led the company's global business for nearly 49 years – Woodruff for 32 years and Goizueta for nearly 17 years until poor health cut short the latter's chequered career and life in 1997. The two TCCC top leaders were great business visionaries and performers. The two extraordinary business thinkers and achievers drove the company's global business ambition, product and market innovation, took its achievements to new heights and helped create the world's most enviable brand.

Between 1997 and 2004, TCCC saw two business leaders in quick succession – Douglas Ivestor and Douglas

N Daft. Ironically, the company's operations and management practices came under heavy criticism across the world during this period. Both Ivestor and Daft resigned as TCCC's chairman-cum-CEO – Ivestor in February 2000 and Daft in May 2004. On 20 February 2004, *Reuters* reported from Atlanta that TCCC Chief Executive Douglas Daft, who had been dogged by government probes, disappointing sales and an anaemic stock price, would retire at the end of 2004. The international wire service quoted the company, as saying that it was open to the idea of considering outside candidates for the top job. Worse news broke on 22 April 2004, when *Wall Street Journal* reported that Gillette CEO James Kilts had taken himself out of the running in Coca-Cola's search for a new chairman and chief executive 'for his own reasons'. It is surprising that over a century old mega-corporation should find the need to hire outside talent to lead itself in the twenty-first century.

Between 1992 and 2003, Coke's India operations had as many as four CEOs. They were: Jaidev Raja, Richard Nicholas, Donald Short and Alexander von Behr. The fifth one, Sanjiv Gupta, joined in 2003. Although the India business has yet to fully stabilize and its bottling operations, which witnessed a very rough journey through 2003, have yet to see profits, CEOs have gone through the turnstiles in rapid succession. Therefore, it is not unnatural for an incumbent to blame his predecessor for the company's problems. The India Division's records with regard to retention of talent and its ability to carry the top management team along are among the most dismal in the annals of the management of large industrial enterprises in the country. Coke's India business heads left even before they had fully settled down. Some left leaving their assignments half-done. For instance, the equity divestment commitment in HCCB was made by Donald Short, but it was completed by his successor, Alex von Behr. Such short-term appointments of business heads also, in a way, affected internal management control and the morale of mid-career and senior management personnel, many of whom had been lured by the company's global brand image. The business heads were often controlled by their direct reporting managers; who, in turn, oversaw the line managers. With short-term objectives, business bosses rarely fiddled with the system or disturbed the arrangement.

While this attitude helped a country manager leave his post without much hassle, the system was corrupted by local function heads, with divided responsibility and conflicting agendas, wielding unchallenged power. Inside Coca-Cola India, the questions that had haunted many in 2004 were: why did Coke wait for the government's order to improve the quality of its water and beverages? Why did Coke challenge the NGO if its product quality deserved improvement? As an industry leader and a global company, why did Coke dither on following the best technical and operational practices? Who was at fault – the technical head or the operations head? What was the role of the division president? Unfortunately, many former senior Coca-Cola India executives say that the India business is beset as much by internal conflicts and controversies as external issues. If lack of stability at the top, focus on individuals than on a team, serious internal allegations concerning integrity and business morality of some of the top functionaries, leading to internal investigations, are regarded as some of the most demoralizing features in any troubled business enterprise, Coke's India operations was riddled by all of them.

Coke's India operations alone were not making regular front-page media stories for the wrong reasons. Senior Coca-Cola India executives were also under constant media glare for one sensational act or the other, attracting investigations into their alleged involvement in various crimes by law enforcement agencies such as the police and Enforcement Directorate. The names of senior Coca-Cola executives were linked to a celebrity murder in a nightclub, and a suicide in a five-star hotel by an estranged daughter-in-law of one of India's former Minister of External Affairs, damaging the image of the brand.

The most surprising development inside the company took place after the India Division won TCCC's prestigious Woodruff Cup, instituted in the memory of the company's longest serving CEO Robert Woodruff, for the division's excellent performance in three key areas – volume, profitability and quality in 2002. The Cup was awarded in 2003. TCCC's global operations covering nearly 200 countries are distributed among 24 divisions. These divisions are divided into two categories. The top category comprises matured, high volume and strategic markets such as North America, Europe, Japan and Mexico. The second category consists of emerging markets and low volume, low profit countries. Within months of receiving the Cup, Coke's Team India 2002 nearly disintegrated with as many as five top functionaries representing the division's regional operations, and heads of legal and information service functions quitting the company. Several mid-level executives from various functions also left the India operations. The company lost a number of senior executives between 2002 and 2004, including seven vice presidents, all top performers with excellent credentials. One of them left the India Division only to resurface a year later as a senior executive in another Coke division in another part of Asia. Did Coke institute an independent enquiry into the exodus of such senior management personnel within such a short period, or did it close the issue after the routine exit interviews?

Like an individual, a good company not only does a good job, but also inspires self-esteem by being upright and honest itself. Independent internal investigations into irregularities and allegations are important management tools employed by every democratic institution, including corporate entities in order to come clean before both internal and external audiences. Though Coke's India operations are comparatively new, it had instituted several internal investigations ranging from operational bungling to violation of Code of Business Conduct (COBC) involving top-level executives. The results of some of these enquiries were believed to have established irregularities by Coke employees. Yet, not all offenders were treated as per the TCCC's rule book. Junior executives involved were handed down harsh punishments. Some lost jobs. Others were transferred. But the big ones managed to get away lightly. These cases involved violation of currency regulations, concealment of vital pre-entry information regarding earlier job acceptance with rival PepsiCo India, sexual harassment of a female brand ambassador, and so on. In most of these cases, the charges were either not pursued or withdrawn, but they often projected a negative image of high-profile Coke executives, tarnishing the image of the company and its brand reputation. Surprisingly, the company itself appeared to be little concerned about the continuous negative media publicity surrounding its senior executives. These reports did not lead to any serious internal scrutiny to determine whether the executives were involved. The Coke management was not known to have issued any warning to such free-wheeling executives about the need to maintain an honourable personal profile in public places. Ironically, most of these individuals were decorated by the company with promotions, higher responsibilities and plum postings abroad, sending wrong signals to other executives in the organization.

Since 1998, Coke's India business was replete with internal management squabbles, and allegations and counter allegations on various fronts. During this period two specific issues concerning the code of business ethics shook the internal management structure of the company as both the cases were widely discussed among managers at all levels within the company. Both the issues surfaced in the year 2000. One concerned huge irregularities in Coke's north India operations and the other related to the appointment of marketing consultants. In the first case, the violations reached such proportions that the company had to appoint an outside firm, erstwhile Arthur Andersen, to investigate operational practices, including financial management in the region. The division's statutory auditors are Ernst & Young. The assignment to Arthur Andersen covered issues such as discounts and schemes, sale by distributors, glass on loan to customers, premia items used for promotional purposes, settlement process and contract labour.

The Arthur Andersen report pointed to the appointment of fake distributors, fudging of sales figures, appointment of a super distributor for Varanasi city on extremely soft terms, misapplication of cash and checks, misappropriation of cash collections and violation of credit and incentive norms. While the company took action against erring individuals, mostly junior and middle level managers, the investigation was reportedly dropped just when it started moving upward.

The second case involved a two-member internal investigation against a senior company executive about certain marketing related transactions Coke's India Division had entered into with a firm called Great Savers Marketing Pvt. Limited, which was owned by his immediate family members. The members of the internal investigation team were Coca-Cola India's then Chief Financial Officer (CFO), Gabe Pataky and legal affairs head, Joel Peres. The issue was 'conflict of interest' – violation of the COBC – by this senior executive. The investigation was directed by Atlanta under the leadership of one of TCCC's high-profile executives, Steve Vondehaar, who was known for his high level of integrity and commitment to the global company's COBC across the Coke system. The internal investigation made some interesting revelations. Within months of the concerned executive's joining Coca-Cola India in its marketing function in October 1997, the company sponsored a direct mailer brought out by little known Great Savers Marketing, initially in Delhi and later in Mumbai. The marketing firm was incorporated in June 1997 and promoted by two sisters of the Coke executive in question. The firm had reportedly received tens of lakhs of rupees from Coca-Cola India between 1998 and 2000. Its indirect business benefits were immense because of its association with the world's biggest brand, Coca-Cola. While the investigative team felt the concerned executive violated the company's COBC and favoured the termination of his job, the division president held a different view. Ultimately, he was let-off lightly. The executive concerned later held a key position within the Coke system.

Incidents of nepotism are not unique to Indian business conditions. Nor are they unique to Indian bottling operations of TCCC, which have been under pressure for incurring continuous losses and huge write-offs. Even the management of the parent company, TCCC has been accused of fudging shipments of concentrates and window dressing financial statements. During 2004, US regulators subpoenaed the company's employees during a federal probe into the business ethics of the world's largest soft drink manufacturer. The US attorney's office and the Securities and Exchange Commission (SEC) were examining whether TCCC over-shipped soft drink concentrate to distributors in some markets, including Japan, thereby possibly inflating financial results. The operational practice is popularly called 'channel stuffing' and refers to a murky legal manner in which a firm convinces its clients to accept unwanted or early deliveries of a product, often offering special incentives and using its predominant position in the market. The method is used to inflate revenues and help meet quarterly financial targets. US media said three former finance executives of the company had informed federal investigators that Coke had engaged in 'channel stuffing' in Japan in recent years. Interestingly, the methods applied to such a business practice are somewhat similar to those pointed out in the Arthur Andersen report on irregularities in Coke's Indian bottling operations in the northern region. They include rebates, extended payment terms and other incentives provided to clients.

In an unrelated case, also in 2004, the global non-alcoholic beverage major came under fire from Calpers, the California State Pension Fund, and Institutional Shareholder Services, an influential advisory group, which opposed the re-election of one of TCCC's most high-profile directors on its board, complaining of conflict of interest. It was alleged that at least two of the companies belonging to the concerned director do business with Coke. Although the motion failed at TCCC's annual general meeting in April 2004, the dissidents garnered a notable 16 per cent support.

In 1998, rival PepsiCo India levelled a sensational allegation against Coke charging its India operations with 'tortuous interference' by inducing en bloc resignation of its employees and filed a petition before the Delhi High Court. PepsiCo's legal action against Coca-Cola India received wide media coverage all over the country. PepsiCo alleged that Coca-Cola India tried to disrupt its operations by offering 'illegal inducement' to its marketing consultants, senior executives, franchisee employees, distributors and institutional retailers. Consequently, PepsiCo said groups of its employees had begun to leave the company in violation of contractual obligations that required a minimum three-month notice period and a 12-month gap before they could join rival Coke. The PepsiCo petition said 66 key employees of its new bottler in Goa left to join Coke the day the latter began distribution operations. PepsiCo's distributions in Bangalore in southern India and Ahmedabad in the western part of the country had also been similarly targeted. An entire sales team in Kanpur in north India was persuaded to join Coke without any notice. PepsiCo alleged that Coke had thrown 'piles of cash' at several key institutional customers to woo them into its fold. The company sought an injunction from the court to restrain Coca-Cola India from 'offering employment to, or inducing any employees of PepsiCo India to breach existing employment contracts and interfering with the business'.

The PepsiCo petition said that Coke had lured a person who had accepted an appointment letter from the company for the second most important position in the marketing department by offering a higher position in the company. Interestingly, an affidavit filed in the court by Coke in response clearly stated that it had no knowledge about the person concerned having earlier accepted the PepsiCo job. Although from the legal point of view such corporate poaching of people from a rival organization may not be a serious offence, it certainly raises the question of integrity of employees who succumb to blandishments from the competition. Maybe, Coke does not attach much importance to integrity or considers the cliché old fashioned. Coca-Cola India, in its counter presentation before the Delhi High Court, said PepsiCo had suppressed facts in its petition seeking an injunction against Coke for inducing defection of Pepsi's staff, consultants and business associates. The court did not grant an interim injunction against Coke.

14

Not The Real Thing

Whatever be the brand value of Coca-Cola, its reluctant response to the public outcry against its Kerala operations and quality compliance of its products like Kinley water and CSD in India, the disastrous Dasani water launch in the UK in the winter of 2004 and the growing arrogance of the management towards its detractors have taken the fizz out of the company.

The recent 'mocking accusation' in the British media from 'Coca-Cola's detractors' that 'it is not the real thing' after what they found in the much touted Dasani bottled water may be an example of growing consumer and public distrust of the beverage behemoth and its much hyped brands. The company had no choice but to recall some half a million bottles of Dasani water and abandon the sale, at least for some time. Commenting on the incident, *The Observer* painted a painful picture of the company and the attitude of its management. It was best summed up by an observation from a London-based marketing analyst, Allyson Stewart-Allen, 'who was born in North America and studied the rise of Coke. Stewart-Allen said, "Coke is a marketing company. Customers drink the image of youth and vigour it creates. Anything that threatens that image strikes at the company's future – and you don't get much more threatening than selling tap water which turns out to be an expensive disaster". The question raised is, "How could a feel-good firm that boasts 2,000 customers a second [...] create so much bad feeling?" If this is not arrogance, what is? The company does not seem to care about what its consumers, customers and stakeholders feel about it anywhere in the world. Its ways of doing business in a developing country such as India, with much less concern for health and conservation, pliable administration and easy-going regulatory authorities, is even worse. In the UK, Coke at least paid for Thames water, however, small the amount may be compared with the final price of the bottled water. In India, groundwater, which the company exploits without any restriction, comes free.

If the pesticides controversy and the company's constant quarrel with the community in Kerala caused only small embarrassment to TCCC, the management was totally exposed over the Dasani bottled water fiasco in the UK. The product recall from the UK market is somewhat reminiscent of a similar action the company was earlier forced to take in Belgium and France after detection of an overdose of carbon dioxide in Coke making consumers sick. Dasani was not produced 'from some idyllic rural spring' in Scotland or at some other locations in the UK. Coke's bottled drinking water came straight 'from processed tap water in Sidcup, Kent'. It was the biggest marketing farce in memory.

Surprisingly, the company appeared to be oblivious to or unconcerned about the growing public wrath against its questionable practices and claims. It seemed to respond only to mass action (Kerala), class action (allegation of racial discrimination in the US) and actions taken by regulatory authorities and the judiciary. The pattern of its reaction to external criticism and holding statements were archaic, of the mid twentieth century vintage. The statements were evasive, clumsy and often irrelevant, perhaps deliberately so, and out of sync with the times. They made the company and its management instantly untrustworthy and evoked greater inquisitiveness about the company's operations and management practices among its detractors. This kept Coke constantly in the news for one bad reason or the other.

The dictatorial nature of the management did not seem to encourage contrary views or ideas within the organization. Thus, Coke became increasingly prone to crises, many of which were avoidable. In India, Coke ignored the early warning when the pesticides controversy first broke in February 2003, over its Kinley water brand; six months later, it plunged into a deeper crisis over its CSD. While the pesticides controversy was raging throughout the country, the company was constantly in the news for selling products past their expiry dates. At the end of 2003, nearly 1,000 cases against the company were said to be pending before various consumer courts, mostly relating to product quality and the company's integrity. The company did not seem to care. Under constant pressure of pushing sales volume and higher margins, other business considerations were often blurred. The volume pushers called the shots. They were the company's blue-eyed boys. Other management functions were support functions. As a result, the volume pushers were always right. They were part of all other management functions and manipulated them whenever they were in trouble or trapped for wrongdoing. And then, Coke's famous 'incident management and crisis resolution (IMCR)' team got into the act. The company did not change its ways. In the summer of 2004, several thousands of cases of over six-month-old Coke products, all beyond their expiry dates, were confiscated from a small single location at Jammu in north India by the state government. The raid on Coke's warehouses was reported in the Indian media. During the year, a government order forced Coke to upgrade the quality of its bottled drinking water, after the company stoutly defended its pesticide residue content, claiming that it met the EU norms for almost a year.

The basic character of the Coca-Cola management is the same across the world. This is only to be expected of a global company of Coke's age, image and experience. Depending upon the location of its operations, nature of the market and the strength of the regulatory authorities and administration, the management may act differently (Douglas Daft's 'think local, act local'), but the difference is only in degree and not in content. As a result, its corporate reputation has often suffered. The company relies on a short public memory and an advertising and marketing blitz to counter the situation. Dasani was withdrawn from the UK market, within weeks of its launch, after dangerous chemicals were detected in the product and the UK media came down heavily on Coke for its misleading claim that it used a 'NASA-approved reverse osmosis multi-barrier filtration system' for purification of the bottled water. *The Guardian* carried a huge full four-column front page story in its edition of 20 March 2004, with a headline that screamed 'Things get worse with Coke' under a shoulder that read: Off the shelf bottled tap water withdrawn after cancer scare. The accompanying picture showed a blue Dasani bottle upside down with the caption that read: 'Watery grave? The launch of Dasani has proved a disaster for Coca-Cola'. *The Guardian* story said 'the entire UK supply of Dasani was pulled off the shelves because it has been contaminated with bromate, a cancer-causing chemical. So now the full scale of Coke's PR disaster is clear. It goes something like this: take Thames Water from the tap in your factory in Sidcup, Kent; put it through a purification process, call it "pure" and give it a mark-up from 0.03p to 95p per half litre; in the process, add a batch of calcium chloride, containing bromide, for "taste profile"; then pump ozone through it, oxidising the bromide – which is not a problem – into bromate – which is. Finally, dispatch to the shops bottles of water containing up to twice the legal limit for bromate (10 micrograms per litre)', the newspaper's consumer affairs correspondent Felicity Lawrence reported. The interesting part is: a principal inspector for the Drinking Water Inspectorate told *The Guardian* correspondent that he 'checked Thames water's supply [the same] morning and it [was] free of bromate'. The same day *The Guardian* editorial on 'Busted brands' called it a 'double disaster' for Coke and suggested: 'May be it should relaunch the product as what it really is: Thames On Tap, pride of London. At least then it will not fall foul of the trade descriptions act'. The 'holding statement' from the company was typical. Coca-Cola said 'it was voluntarily withdrawing Dasani bottles from the shelf "to ensure that only products of the highest quality are provided to our consumers"'. Does this statement sound familiar in the context of pesticide residue controversy involving Coca-Cola's Kinley water in India among others in the early 2003? The only difference is that the company did not withdraw Kinley, which became India's largest selling bottled drinking water brand in 2002. Instead, it stepped up the manufacturing and sale of the product till 31 December 2003, after which it had no choice but to comply with the improved quality norms under a mandatory executive order of the Indian government. The executive order came into force in January 2004. Coke used the opportunity to raise the prices of Kinley for both the retail and bulk packs for various markets to make its consumers pay for improved quality. So much for Coke's concern for quality and consumers!

The end result of the Kinley water controversy in India in 2003 and the Dasani episode in the UK in 2004 also aptly describe the divergent tales of the two countries on nearly similar issues. The controversy apart, the company in India was richer by an undisclosed sum (sales volume and profit figures of Coke's India operations are kept a 'top secret' as the company takes shelter under 'no public disclosure requirement' for 'private limited' entities as per the Companies Act) from its continued sale of Kinley. Coke paid little attention to the NGO reports. On the contrary, in the UK, 'the Dasani scandal had left Coke nursing a £25 million' hole in its pocket 'from cancelled production contracts and advertising deals. The damage to the firm's reputation, [according to analysts, was] 20 times' the amount, or £500 million.

Few will disagree that the real strength of the low value products of the Coca-Cola company is its high cost advertising and marketing. The company is all about the brand. And, the brand is all about the company. For nearly 100 years, the company directed its marketing focus on a single brand, Coke. The diversification was mainly in terms of variants of Coke. Understandably, the company finds itself most comfortable with marketing its CSDs, which also include popular global brands such as Fanta and Sprite, than other products. Coke's current US $70 billion brand image was crafted over the years in the last century by management maestros Robert Woodruff, J Paul Austin and Roberto Goizueta. However, things changed since the early 1990s, when the company started product diversification in a big way in keeping with the market trend in the US, Europe and Japan and changing consumer preference for juices, health drinks, energy drinks, milk-based drinks, ready-to-serve coffee and tea, low-cost powdered drink and water. During this period, the company has launched over 300 non-cola drinks and several brands of bottled water in some 200 countries. Globally, bottled water has become the fastest growing business, particularly since 2000. The CSD portfolio continues to be the most profitable and the bread-and-butter business for TCCC. Although its Georgia brand coffee is a huge success in Japan and its non-CSD products like 100 per cent juice (Minute Maid), sports drink (Powerade) and bottled water (Dasani) are a big hit in the US and a few other markets, the mindset of the company's top brass is still CSD or, more specifically, Coke-centric. They want to extend the marketing and operational success of the CSD business to other diversified products and brands. In India, Coke's much hyped experiment with non-CSD products like an energy drink, powdered drink and ready-to-serve tea and coffee have so far proved to be a flop. All these products and brands owe their identity to the fact that they are part of the mother brand, Coca-Cola. That has not proved to be a great advantage in India. Many are allergic to the controversy ridden cola brand which has yet to acquire a high percentage of consumers share of throats and continues to remain in the distant third position in the Indian CSD market, more than a decade after it relaunch.

The rigid mindset of the Coca-Cola management is best exemplified in Daft's letter to the company's executives across the world before the Christmas of 2003. He said: 'For nearly 75 years, our company sold a single product: Coca-Cola. Our advertising during much of the era showed Coca-Cola as part of variety of activities: at the beach, on the ski slopes, after work, between games. The promise was that Coca-Cola was "the pause that refreshes" during a busy day – that for an active person, Coca-Cola makes good things taste better. While we now offer a wide variety of beverages that suit all lifestyles and occasions, we are still, fundamentally, a refreshment company'. The contradiction comes in the last part of the letter when he talks about the 'company's commitment to Real FUNdamentals of health and nutrition'. To many, linking CSD, long marketed as a fun and passion product, to health and nutrition is a big joke as much as Coke trying to sell bottled tap water as natural mineral water in the UK.

It seems Coke has not learnt any lessons from its recent business crises and the attack in India. If it had, it would have been a little more careful about making wrong claims about the quality and purity of the bottled water Dasani in the UK market. Coke took decades to build its brand, and its globalization did not have the all pervasive influence of Internet Explorer, websites, hundreds of satellite TV channels and 24X7 news channels in almost every key language of the world. If the pathetic condition of the water-starved people of India's Plachimada village, where Coke has a massive water plant, reached the people of the UK, France, Germany, Australia, Singapore, Brazil and Japan faster than it reached Delhi, so did the news of Coke's Dasani disaster in the UK to the people in India. Even a few years ago, it was unthinkable that an incident in a poor Indian village would disrupt proceedings at a giant global company's annual shareholders' meeting in Wilmington, Delaware, leading to the ejection of a protester in the familiar Japanese style. It happened on 22 April 2004, when US human rights activists and protesters accused TCCC of running bottling plants in India that were depleting water supplies in local communities and causing pollution with discharged materials. Coke's corporate image is suffering in many parts of the world, costing the company huge sums to defend itself against its detractors. This is apart from business losses. Not long ago, it had to settle 'a lawsuit brought by black workers in the US' accusing Coke of 'racial discrimination in its [the company's] pay and promotion policies'. In 2003, Coke's 'rigged marketing test involving Burger King, one of Coke's largest customers' in North America, made sensational news the world over. The result: Coke had to issue a 'public apology' and 'pay compensation to Burger King and its franchisees'. In Columbia, Coke and its bottlers have been accused of conspiring with the government to intimidate labour unions at the plants, an allegation that the company has totally denied. Cases have been filed against the company by human rights activists in US courts. The list goes on.

Against this backdrop, Coca-Cola's twenty-first century 'Magna Carta' sounds rather hollow, unreal and unconnected with its ground level actions. The company has failed to fulfil its promise and aspirations which, it said, would drive its decisions and actions for the twenty-first century. It said: 'As each day unfolds, we will take clear, disciplined action against 10 explicit priorities'. These priorities are:

- the company will actively cultivate a diverse, rewarding culture that encourages its people to develop their fullest potential, assuring enjoyment and satisfaction in the Coca-Cola work environment. The company will continue to evolve structures to enable itself to 'think local, act local';
- the company will intensely promote innovation as an explicit priority in every aspect of its business, including its business structures;
- it will seek genuine, trusting relationships with all its constituents. It will focus especially on the people who buy its brands, appealing not only to their shared values, but also to their differences;
- it will rejuvenate the basic brand building nature of the company, with focus on brand Coca-Cola;
- the company will, at the same time, broaden its historical portfolio of brands, products and services;
- it will work with its bottling partners with clear respect for the interdependent nature of its relationship, actively supporting their efforts to evolve business structures that work best for them;
- it will work creatively with those who sell the company's products in the marketplace, developing relationships built on mutual success, not only from its brands, but also from its services;
- the company will develop new alliances with uniquely qualified partners, to tap into emerging growth opportunities and new routes to market;
- it will continually operate as model business citizens, consistently shaping its business decisions to improve

the quality of life in the communities where it does business; and

- it will insist on demonstrating clear leadership and innovation in sustaining the environment, continually collaborating with its suppliers.

If words were substitutes for action, Coke would have no problem with anyone anywhere in the world. A review of its operations in India and other parts of the world since 2000 will show that the company hardly means what it vows. Paradoxically, the community and environment are Coke's last two priorities of action during the current century. For the greater part of 2003, the company was almost under a siege in India because of wrongdoing and not because it ran short of good words in its 'holding statements'. In fact, the company probably produced more words than the number of bottles to hopelessly defend its controversial actions before the public, the government, the regulatory authorities, the judiciary, the JPC and the national and international media. Events that followed indicated that the company did not trust its own words and twisted them at will to extricate itself from sticky situations. Coke's business impairment losses in India are known. Will the company tell its shareholders the cost of its 2003 tussle against the community, NGOs, regulatory authorities, as well as those towards legal actions, social appeasement and management of 'environment' in India? And, what did it achieve?

Going by the way Coke does business in India and other parts of the world, nothing sounds more pompous than the company's promise that 'nothing is more important to our success than integrity. This begins with insisting on absolute quality for every one of our products, and acting with a sense of accountability in everything we do'. In India, it is now official that the company's products were below standard, it guzzled billions of gallons of free groundwater for commerce, it was involved in damaging environment and ecology, it dumped toxic wastes on farmland, it deprived the Indian shareholders of voting rights and, finally, the brand Coca-Cola continues to be a marketing failure. The Coca-Cola of the twenty-first century may not stand for the best American values that it once claimed to represent. Coke seems to be facing the biggest ever identity crisis in India and elsewhere.

Postscript

Douglas Draft's listless innings at the helm of TCCC ended faster than anyone had expected. Daft, an Australian, left TCCC in May 2004, even before he was 60. The company's non-executive board appointed another Coke veteran Neville Isdell as TCCC's chairman-cum-CEO with effect from 1 June 2004. This put at rest the months-long speculation over the company's hunt for an outside talent to protect the world's largest brand and steer the management of the non-alcoholic beverage behemoth. Coke received bad publicity in the US media after Gillette's head made a statement saying he was not available for the top job in Coke. Irishman Isdell, then in his early 60s, was considered to be a rank outsider. He was known to be a great strategist as well as a staunch believer in the company's time tested business model for CSD, its bread and butter. And, it did not come as any surprise to anyone within the company that the new Coke CEO quickly got rid of key members of Daft's team to exercise full control over the company's executive management. Nearly half a dozen top Coke functionaries, including heads of the company's global operations and marketing, left the company within weeks.

Isdell also did not waste time in seeking to review Coke's India operations, which had tarnished its reputation worldwide after the pesticides controversy, mass action against Coke in Kerala, constant fights with NGOs in several parts of the country over excessive exploitation of groundwater and dumping of industrial wastes. The speed with which he moved to assess the messy India business situation surprised even those who had known him for years. Daft had not found the time to visit India to assess the situation personally even once during the last three years when the local subsidiary went through extremely troubled times because of growing public discontent over the company's operational style and NGO bashing for ruining the environment. Internally, there were issues like management integrity, operational freedom of various key functions and growing disenchantment among senior executives. Coca-Cola India's local management practices were under constant public attack both in India and abroad for almost two years. Susceptible to sycophancy, bureaucratically oriented Daft probably believed in seeing things through his ears rather than eyes. Unreal questions and answers, constantly revised holding statements, paper strategies and tactics and highly impressive PowerPoint presentations kept Atlanta happy. Occasional visitors from Atlanta, overseeing operations in Asia and Occania, were received with such pomp and show that it would have made even a very level-headed person gloss over the dark spots under the lamp.

Isdell's immediate action gave an impression that the company would be more watchful about the way the country heads ran their businesses and exercised more control over troubled markets and troubled regions.

Barely three weeks into his new role as the master of the world's biggest brand, Isdell managed to spend several valuable hours in Delhi to personally review the India Division operations. Incidentally, Isdell was the person who had not only strategized Coke's re-entry in India, but got Rajan Pillai off its back just in time to launch its wholly owned operations.

While Coke's India Division was tight-lipped about the purpose and outcome of Isdell's lightning trip, an apparently selective media leak suggested that the new Coke CEO was not keen on continuing with the experiment of running vast company owned bottling operations in the country in which it had already invested nearly US $1 billion and had yet to see any profit even after axing a large number of employees under the 'voluntary' retirement scheme in 2001–2 and 2002–3. HCCB's 2001–2 annual report said the voluntary retirement scheme for its employees at Jamshedpur, Najibabad, Dasna, Jaipur, Udaipur, Jammu, Chennai, Nellore and Vijaywada cost the company Rs 10 million.

A media report said that the authorities and powers of the India Division management on the company's bottling operations might be 'significantly curtailed' and added that it 'could be the biggest overhaul of Coca-Cola India's operative model in India'. Isdell was in favour of operating through franchisee bottlers. 'He [had] already identified India as a strategic market and [...] managers of all COBOs [company-owned-botting plants would] report to Irial Finan (global president of bottling operation) [...] beginning August 1, 2004'. These actions could mean a massive restructuring of Coke's bottling operations in India and substantial erosion of the present powerful status of the division head. The key motive behind this move appears to be financial. The Pune-based Coca-Cola India Pvt. Limited has been a highly successful and profit-making enterprise from its very inception. HCCB is the problem.

Obviously, Isdell's strategy was to make the company's India bottling operations profitable as quickly as possible while insulating the brand Coke from public ire through deeper involvement of local franchisees in its bottling operations. But this is easier said than done. It could effectively mean that Coke reverts to its earlier business model of serving the Indian market through regional anchor bottling companies under the operational leadership of franchisee partners. HCCB will have to be split into several companies or demerge into four or five corporate entities. And, for this, it will have to find new local suitors.

HCCB has been the single biggest headache for the parent company. It is also the public face of Coke's India operations. The bottling company has failed in all its financial performance projections. Even in the year it divested its shares, it could not keep its promise about profitability. HCCB's annual report and audited accounts for 2001–2 emphatically mentioned that 'we hope the company would be able to break even at the end of the current year (2002–3)'. The bottling company's 2002–3 audited accounts continued to show operating losses. Worse still, its wholly owned subsidiary, Hindustan Coca-Cola Marketing Company Pvt. Limited, incurred huge losses during the year. Coke's little known marketing company suffered a loss of over Rs 1,920 million against a gross income of Rs 16.28 billion. The marketing company was brought into operation in 2000–1 with a paid up capital of only Rs 20. It was subsequently raised to Rs 1,000 with 100 equity shares of Rs 10 each. At the end of March 2003, it had 10,100 equity shares of Rs 10 each. Daft might not have been fully briefed about this heavy loss-making marketing company before Coca-Cola India was chosen for the Woodruff Award, but it was unlikely to have been missed by a more careful Isdell.

The performance of Coke's India bottling operations continued to be very poor in the following areas. HCCB's sales turnover in 2003–4 was only Rs 13,310.44 million and it incurred a net loss of Rs 4,560.63 million. In 2004–5, the sales turnover improved only marginally to Rs 13,561.81 million and the year's net loss went up to Rs 5,390.25 million. The Hindustan Coca-Cola Marketing Company, a subsidiary, showed equally poor financials during this period. The marketing company's net loss in 2003–4 was Rs 1,270.7 million as against a turnover of Rs 6,068.3 million. Its losses, however, came down to Rs 844.8 million on a marginally higher turnover of Rs 6,242.4 million, the following year.

HCCB's financial performance had been so bad that Coke's existing franchisee bottlers were least inclined to acquire HCCB shares and become a useful partner of the bottling company, which was in a way also their competitor. The company's business assets were highly overvalued because of the historical factor with equally high overhead costs. These bottlers showed little interest in HCCB's local equity issue on a preferential basis. It is fairly common knowledge that some of Coke's sticky bottling assets are located in water-starved areas in the states of Kerala, Rajasthan, Maharashtra and Madhya Pradesh. Coke's prospective franchisee bottlers are unlikely to ignore the historical perspective and the recent developments before jumping into a fresh business alliance with the company.

TCCC may be capable of sorting out the issues related to India business restructuring to streamline its bottling operations and stop them from bleeding. Atlanta feels that its bottling subsidiary in India is finally on the right track. HCCB will start making profit from 2008. But that does not automatically take care of the ill will the company has generated among the community and social activists. One would be more interested to know Isdell's strategy to address the water scarcity and environmental issues while the huge water plants dig deep into the earth to pump out millions of gallons of precious groundwater to produce beverages and packaged drinking water. Technology can take care of the quality of beverages and water bottled by Coke. Strict adherence to ethical standards may help deal with the problem of supplying products to the market after their expiry period. It may try to change its product profile and marketing strategy for greater acceptance among the health conscious. Other issues like disposal of used pet bottles and solid waste management are not insurmountable. But the real challenge before the Coke management is to balance its business priorities with growing social concerns over dwindling water resources.

Much of Coke's future business success in India will depend on the extent to which the company is prepared to respond to the sensitivities of the underprivileged people in the country's remote areas where a large number of the company's groundwater guzzling bottling plants are located. The business success will depend on Coke's willingness to involve the local community before investing in new water plants in the country. The International Finance Corporation (IFC), a commercial lending window of the World Bank, recently told a corporate borrower from India to meet the villagers opposing the company's plan to divert water from a Himalayan stream near Kullu in Himachal Pradesh in order to set up a 192 megawatt hydroelectric project. IFC asked the company, Rajasthan Spinning & Weaving Mills Limited, to conduct an ESIA of the project and hold public consultations with the villagers for their consent. IFC's concern is understandable. Not long ago, World Bank Vice President Ismael Serageldin had predicted that 'if wars of this century [twentieth century] were fought over oil, the wars of next century will be fought over water'. Will Coke follow the IFC model before it sets up new water plants in India to avoid the risk of waging a war against an Indian community and ruining its business forever, in the process?

The brand Coke continues to evoke public distrust and ire. *The Economic Times' Brand Equity* annual survey of India's most trusted brands on 30 May, 2007 ranked Coke 42nd among the top 100 brands. In its 2002 survey, Coke was listed among the top 12 brands and Thums Up was among the top 10. The 2007 *Brand Equity* survey sent Thums Up down to the 37th position while Pepsi ranked 20th. It will be interesting to watch how Isdell and his new team manage to arrest Coke's eroding corporate and brand image in India. It is a stupendous task.

Fortunately, Atlanta is not giving up. Instead, it has already launched an all-out programme to quickly repair the damage and move on. TCCC is fully aware of the challenges ahead as also the growth prospects of its business in India, the economy of which is growing at 9 per cent annually. Coke's Team India has been totally restructured. Atlanta is in full control of HCCB's operations. A number of corrective measures have been taken by the company's operational management in India to spruce up its corporate as well as community image while taking new marketing initiatives for better positioning of its brands.

The company had launched its top selling global 100 per cent juice brand, Minute Maid, in India in 2007. These steps have already started producing results. Coke's 13-year-long bumpy journey through India appears to have ended ultimately in a smooth run. The India operations are finally on the path of steady growth and progress. According to latest reports, Isdell & Company have turned the India operations viable. In 2007, HCCB's accounts were in the black, a situation which was unthinkable even three years ago. The parent company had invested over 1 billion dollars in India since its inception. Coca-Cola has now chalked out a plan to make a fresh investment to the tune of $ 250 million to grow further in the Indian market.

The company seems to have learnt from its past mistakes in dealing with the government, public and NGOs and has chosen to shed its arrogant image to address and not challenge the concern of the society and be transparent in its dealings with the stakeholders. By the end of 2007, Coke decided not to set up any new plant in India without the approval of the local community. Coca-Cola also decided to conduct studies at its existing plants to update the water resources position there and address any problem. It has formally shut down the Plachimada plant in Kerala. As Neville Isdell prepares to retire as Coke's global CEO in 2008, the cola giant has approached India's most high-profile environmental body, New Delhi-based The Energy and Resources Institute (TERI), to conduct an audit of its water practices in India. It is good that Coke has understood, although the hard way, the value of a good corporate citizen image tag. The company is working with Indian farmers for mutual benefit.

While the company has been the largest corporate consumer of Indian sugar and mango pulp, it has also emerged as India's No. 1 coffee exporter. Coke's turbulent times in India seem to have come to an end. The end came almost the way it began nearly two decades ago – with a lot of fanfare and hope. Once again, Edward Neville Isdell made it happen. He was instrumental to the company's return to India as an independent entity after it broke away from Rajan Pillai. Almost 18 years later, Isdell made the company's dream come true by making the India operations a truly large and profitable venture with the focus set strongly on business and not on gimmicks and controversies. On his last visit to India as the company's chairman cum CEO in mid March of 2008, 64-year-old Isdell expressed that his mission was nearly complete. The India operations have turned healthy, profitable and sustainable. He wants India to break into Coke's top ten operations in the world. At the moment, it ranks sixteenth. During his symbolic trip to Agra, where Coke was relaunched 16 years ago, he confessed to a group of media persons that the company, before he took charge in 2004, had become too bureaucratic, too slow in decision-making and the people were not as intimately focused on their jobs as they should have been. It seems Coke has detected the Red Signal finally.

Notes

Chapter 3
RAJAN PILLAI AND COKE
Antoine Riboud's statements regarding the tussle between BSN and Rajan Pillai was reported in the *Business Standard,* 24 November 1992.

Chapter 4
BUSINESS BULLY
The cover story referred to on p.22 is from the *Businessworld,* 24 December 2001.

Chapter 5
LEGAL COBWEB
HCCSW, HCCNW, BCCSE and BCCNE had a common registered office at 13 Abul Fazal Road, Bengali Market, New Delhi 110 001. The suggested amalgamation scheme of the five subsidiaries is a follows:

The scheme said, 'The Coca-Cola Company, USA, the ultimate holding company, indirectly owns seven subsidiaries in India. These are: the transferor company and two other subsidiaries – Hindustan Coca-Cola Holdings Private Limited and Bharat Coca-Cola Holdings Private Limited. Hindustan Coca-Cola Holdings Private Limited in turn has two subsidiaries, HCCNW and HCCSW (Transferee Company), while Bharat Coca-Cola Holdings Private Limited also has two subsidiaries, BCCNE and BCCSE. At the instance of TCCC, the ultimate holding company, the Transferor Company is desirous of consolidating part of its continuing business, referred to in this Scheme as Transferred Undertakings of the Transferor Company especially when three other group companies are amalgamating pursuant to separate proceedings being simultaneously initiated in the Delhi High Court for the merger of HCCNW, BCCSE and BCCNE into HCCSW, the Transferee Company herein.

'The present scheme has been proposed to facilitate management, administration and financial efficiencies, and alignment, coordination and streamlining of day to day running of operations relating to preparation, packaging, sale and distribution of non-alcoholic beverages in the Republic of India with a view to improving cash flows and returns to shareholders on the large investments made and proposed to be made.

'The Transferor Company while continuing its business, on the Scheme being sanctioned, will focus its attention on improving efficiencies for the manufacture and sale of concentrate and beverage bases, and other related operations'.

It was further stated that the amalgamation would create synergies of operations besides economies in administrative and managerial costs by combining operations and this would result in improved performance for the amalgamated transferee company. The amalgamation will improve the financial structure and cash flow management of the transferee company, while combining the manufacturing strengths and reserves of the transferor companies.

Chapter 6
SHARES DISINVESTMENT
A sample of the company's letters to the concerned authorities is as follows:

For instance, as late as 7 November 2002, HCCH came out with a fresh plea seeking the government's approval to convert a part of its investment in HCCB into preference shares. A letter was addressed to the secretary, Department of Industrial Policy and Promotion, Ministry of Industry, Government of India, asking the government to allow the Company to utilize 'part of the total FDI brought into our company and lying as unused balance in the advance against share capital account of HCCB, towards purchase of preference shares in subsidiary Hindustan Coca-Cola Beverages Private Limited'.

The letter said, 'As part of balance sheet restructuring of HCCB, we also reviewed various other financial issues, including the optimum level of capital (equity and preference) and debt equity ratios for HCCB going forward. Based on advice received from our investment bankers and tax advisors and taking into account both, a short and long term view, we determined the size of the equity in HCCB to be Rs 4,05,00,04,080 (Rs 4.05 billion). The total issued and paid up equity share capital in HCCB currently stands at Rs 4,05,00,04,080. Of this, HCCB issued 105,000,000 (one hundred and five million) equity shares of the face value of Rs 10 each, at a premium of Rs 200 per share. An amount of Rs 21 billion accordingly stands in the securities premium account.

'Based on advice from our merchant bankers and in order to be fair to the new investors in HCCB, HCCB decided to set off its accumulated losses of Rs 20.86 billion against the amount of Rs 21 billion standing in the securities premium account and restructure its balance sheet. In order to accomplish this, a petition for reduction of capital was filed in the Delhi High Court under the Companies Act'. To highlight the point that the capital restructuring exercise was a great job undertaken for the benefit of Indian shareholders, the Coke letter had the message in italics: '*This capital reduction will be the largest capital reduction exercise ever undertaken in India and would in effect be equivalent to The Coca-Cola Company having made a foreign equity investment on a non-repatriable basis of Rs 20.86 billion (approx. US $423 million) in India*'.

Elaborating on the capital restructuring programme and the options before the company, Coke wrote:

'Of the total Rs 33,083,596,080 in HCCB:

(i) Rs 4.05 billion represent equity capital (issued and paid up);

(ii) Rs 21 billion stands in the securities premium account (against which total accumulated losses of Rs 20.86 billion will be set off pursuant to the sanction of the High Court on the petition for reduction of capital) – a balance of Rs 140 million will then remain in the securities premium account);

(iii) The balance of Rs 8,033,592,000 will remain unutilised in the advance against share capital account.

Our company has the option of repatriating the said amount of Rs 8,033,592,000 (which was originally brought in as FDI on a repatriable basis);

Or

Subject to appropriate no-objection/approval, utilise the said amount in India through investment in preference shares in our subsidiary HCCB;

To repatriate the said amount and subject to appropriate approvals from government:

(a) Bring the said amount back as an external commercial borrowing (ECB) to finance HCCBs business in India; or
(b) Bring the said amount back as FDI into India on a repatriable basis for investment by our company in preference shares in HCCB.

'So as not to send any negative signals, our company has decided not to repatriate the said amount of Rs 8,033,592,000, but instead seeks approval for our company to invest the said amount in preference shares in HCCB.

'The approvals granted to our company r/w (read with) the subsequent amendment letters did not prohibit an investment in preference shares in HCCB or the issuance of preference shares by HCCB to our company (the requirement which was stating the obvious, was that the investment by our company in HCCB was to be in Indian rupees). Out of abundant caution, we are making this application to seek no objection/approval of the government to use the investment made by our company in HCCB which is lying as advance against share capital in the books of HCCB, towards investment in redeemable, non-cumulative, non-participating preference shares of HCCB. These preference shares would be issued by HCCB as fully paid up at their face value as Rs 10 per share and carry a dividend of 1 per cent of the face value per annum, and would be redeemed in one instalment at the expiry of seven years from the date of allotment'.

The Coca-Cola press statement referred to on p.35 was released on 16 August 2002.

Chapter 7

THE POOR THIRD

The information on p.45 about The Coca-Cola Company's carbonated soft drinks business is sourced from the company's 2001 Annual Report.

Chapter 8

THINK LOCAL, ACT LOCAL

The author was among those who were presented the *Red Book* – a vision statement of the The Coca-Cola Company for the twenty-first century presented by Douglas Daft. The provisions of the PFA Act regarding carbonated water referred to in the chapter are:

According to the PFA Act, Section A01.01, 'Carbonated water means potable water integrated with carbon dioxide under pressure and may contain any of the following singly or in combination. Sugar, liquid glucose, dextrose monohydrate, invert sugar, fructose, sorbitol, honey, fruit and vegetable extractives and permitted flavouring, colouring matter, preservatives, emulsifying and stabilising agents, acids (citric acid, fumaric acid, tartaric acid, phosphoric acid, lactic acid, ascorbic acid and malic acid), edible gums (such as guar, karaya, arabic, carobean, furcellaran, tragacanth, gum ghatti, edible gelatin, albumin, licorice and its derivatives), salt of sodium, calcium and magnesium, vitamins, caffeine'. Carbonated water constitutes a common list of additives. It 'includes the beverages which comply with the definition, which utilise these additives and which do not claim to be a part of adjacent categories such as fruit juices and nectars, dairy drinks, mineral waters, etc'.

The story on advertisements defacing Himalayan rocks was carried by the Sunday edition of *The Indian Express,* 11 August 2002.

Chapter 9

COKE AND CONTROVERSY

The IUPAC Commission's recommendations referred to on p.62 are sourced from:

'Regulatory Limits For Pesticide Residues In Water', (IUPAC Technical Report), *Pure and Applied Chemistry,* Vol. 75, No. 8, 2003.

The recommendations of the IUPAC Commission on Agrochemicals and the Environment are:

1. 'The terminology for pesticide residue limits in water should be harmonized. As a first step, IUPAC should prepare and issue

recommended terminology for the various limits and guidelines for pesticide residues in water. International agencies and national governments would then be encouraged to adopt the terminology when introducing or revising their regulations or recommendations.

2. The aim or purpose of establishing a set of pesticide residue limits in water should be clearly enunciated so that they are only used for the intended purpose.
3. The nature of the water to which the pesticide residue limits apply should be defined and explained.
4. The methods for establishing pesticides residue limits in water should be described and should include the data requirements, assumptions, reasons for choice of factors (assessment, uncertainty or safety) and the nature of the water to which the limits apply.
5. The rationale for each pesticide residue limit should be explained publicly in a transparent way. The explanation should summarize the available data, draw attention to inadequacies or inconsistencies of data and show in a logical way the derivation of the recommended value. The explanation should include, where relevant, the choice of factor (assessment, uncertainty or safety), availability of analytical methods, and residue definition.
6. The compound or compounds to be included in a residue limit for water should be stated. It is preferable to set individual residue limits for parent pesticide and each relevant transformation product.
7. Analytical methods for residues in water should be developed with limits of quantification (LOQs) low enough to match concentrations related to relevant biological effects.
8. A pesticide residue limit in water that is designed for monitoring or regulatory purposes should be established at a level no lower than the LOQ of a practical analytical method.
9. A process designed to reduce the levels of pesticide residues in water should not introduce contaminants that pose new risks.
10. Guidelines for drinking water calculated from acceptable daily intake (ADI) should follow the WHO system [60-kg body weight, consumption 2l/day, allocate 1 or 10% toler-able daily intake (TDI) or ADI depending on the pesticide uses and properties].

11. Guideline levels should never be taken as a licence to degrade a water supply to the guideline levels.
12. Short-term deviations above a regulatory limit for residues in water do not necessarily mean that the water is unsuit-able for the intended purpose. The amount and duration of the deviation should be subject to a risk assessment taking into account the basis for the regulatory limit.'

Coke's advertisement appeared in the Delhi edition of the *Hindustan Times*, 8 February 2003. The company claimed: 'The brand meets the internationally accepted and used World Health Organization guidelines for potable drinking water. To ensure that every drop of Kinley water we bring to you is absolutely safe, these are the stringent quality and safety norms we follow:

1. Every Kinley bottle and jar (bulk pack) that leaves our international standard, state-of-the-art plants conforms to international WHO guidelines (WHO, Edition 2) and the highest Indian standard, BIS (IS 14543:1998).
2. Every drop that reaches you goes through a seven-step purification process, which includes:
   - Reverse Osmosis – Removes contaminants as minute as 0.000001mm – the best available technology across the world for water treatment
   - Chlorination – Disinfects water
   - Multi-layered filtration – Removes suspended particles and other odour and taste causing compounds
   - Granular activated carbon purification – Effectively removes organic, colouring and off-taste and odour-causing compounds
   - Mineral injection – Reconstitutes water with desirable minerals required by the human body
   - Micron filtration
   - Ozonation – Ensures destruction of any micro-organism and also disinfects water
3. 100 per cent of the Kinley water we manufacture goes through a state-of-the-art reverse osmosis water treatment system that removes substances as small as 0.000001mm (the smallest bacterium is 0.0002mm), and/or particles even as minute as atoms.

4. We test for traces of pesticide in groundwater to the level of parts per million (which is equivalent to one drop in a million drops) as per BIS (14543:1998) and WHO guidelines (Vol. 1, Edition 2). Even at those stringent miniscule levels, nothing has been detected in Kinley water. Therefore, we can safely assert that there is no contamination or toxicity whatsoever in packaged Kinley water. Drinking packaged Kinley water is and will be safe during your entire lifetime.
5. As a statement of our total belief, we would like to say that today all employees of Coca-Cola India, our families, our children and loved ones, proudly consume the Kinley water that we serve you.
6. As a committed corporate citizen and global socially responsible company, we have and will always ensure compliance with the laws of the land and globally accepted and used guidelines of the WHO.
7. As a reinforcement of our conviction, we welcome you to visit any of our international, state-of-the-art manufacturing plants to witness with what care we bring you Kinley packaged drinking water. We are confident you will trust it 100 percent.'

Chapter 10

PESTICOLA

The Centre for Science and Environment (CSE), the NGO which made public the levels of pesticide residues in soft drinks.

All the quotations in this chapter are from:

'Coke, Pepsi fizz with pesticides, says study', *The Times of India*, 5 August 2003.'Poison in your soft drink: Study', *Hindustan Times*, 5 August 2003, 'Coca-Cola's bottled water is from the tap', *Times Online*, 1 March 2004, 'Coca-Cola's special water source is a tap in Sidcup', *The Daily Telegraph*, 2 March 2004, 'Pepsi, Coke Censured in India. Report Confirms Pesticide Findings of Environmental Group', *The Washington Post*, 5 February 2004.

The advertisement, 'Coca-Cola manufactures World Class & Safe products in India' was published in the Delhi edition of the *Hindustan Times*, 7 August 2003. While trying to rubbish the NGO's claims of high pesticides levels in Coca-Cola, Fanta, Sprite, Thums Up and Limca, Coke's advertisement said:

- Recent reports on soft drinks released by Centre for Science and Environment (CSE), are incorrect & baseless.
- The soft drinks manufactured in India conform to the same high standards of quality as in USA & Europe. There is no duality of standards.
- Our Quality Systems and Standards are international & we use state of the art technology to ensure the same in India. We stringently test our soft drinks at International, independent and accredited laboratories in India and abroad. We have results from TNO Nutrition and Food Research Lab, Netherlands, that testify that the water used in our beverages is totally safe. TNO of Netherlands is an accredited and world renowned top grade laboratory. It is accredited on ISO 17025 standard which is recognised as the GOLD standard in testing/ analysis. The results are completely open for any governmental agency/regulator to inspect. These can be reviewed on www.myenjoyzone.com and www.hungama.com.
- Stringent quality monitoring takes place for both the source water and finished products. We test for traces of pesticides in ground water to the level of parts per billion (which is equivalent to one drop in a billion drops). Illustratively, it translates to measuring one second in 32 years, or less than one person in the entire population in India. These tests require specialised equipment at accredited labs to have accurate results. TNO is one such lab. Even at these stringent miniscule levels we are well within the internationally accepted norms.
- Therefore we can safely assert that there is no contamination or toxicity whatsoever in our brand of beverages. Drinking our beverages is and will be safe & refreshing during your entire lifetime.
- Quality you can trust – As a statement of our total belief, we would like to say that all our 5,000 employees of Coca-Cola India, our families, our children and loved ones, proudly consume our soft drinks that we serve you.

- More than a billion times everyday, in over 200 countries across the globe, consumers choose our brand of refreshment because Coca-Cola is a symbol of Quality.
- Our promise to deliver the highest quality product every day makes us the most valuable brand in the world.

  As a reinforcement of our conviction, we welcome you to visit any of our manufacturing plants to witness the absolute care with which we manufacture our brands of beverages. We are confident you will trust us.

  Quality... Trust... That's Our Promise.

The statement made by Sushma Swaraj, Minister of Health and Family Welfare and Parliamentary Affairs in the Lok Sabha is from 'Sushma clarifies on soft drinks', *The Hindu*, 22 August 2003. CFTRI's observation on p.91 is available on the CSE's website [http://www.cseindia.org/html/cola-indepth/CFL_Report.PDF].

The quotation on p.94 is compiled from the EU's own website [http://europa.eu.int], the Coke communication said: 'compared to water, the maximum residue limits (MRL) of lindane in milk and cream was 10 times higher, DDT 400 times and chlorpyrifos 100 times. Egg in shell carried 1,000 times more lindane than water, 500 times more DDT and 100 times more chlorpyrifos. Compared with water, bovine meat carried 200 times more lindane, 10,000 times more DDT and 500 times more chlorpyrifos. In the case of apple, the respective variations are 100 times, 500 times and 5,000 times, in addition to 5,000 times more malathion (a pesticide which was not mentioned for three other categories). In fact, the total MRL content in apple was 1.54 lakh times more than the comparable EU norm for water. The Coke docket meant for "public education" feared that the adoption of EU norms in India could result in:

- India importing basic food stuffs/cereals to meet EU food safety standards.
- Closure of our dairy sector until all cattle is only machine milked.
- Ninety per cent of our groundnut crop would become inedible due to aflatoxin standards.
- No 'whisky' production locally unless from malted grain.

- Packaging standards raising the cost of most basic necessities significantly.
- Huge financial impact on the economy at large.
- The company even went a step further calling for prudence and scientific debate on the application of EU norms in India. It said: "Adopting 'foreign' standards needs to be assessed fully in both qualitative and quantitative terms".
- Standards are dynamic and must evolve to address market needs and India's own competitiveness.
- Protecting the health and safety of consumers in India is a fundamental role of the Government of India. This duty can be responsibly discharged.
- The Indian consumer's expectation is that standards will inform the consumer and instil confidence in products developed to that standard.
- There is no European Union monopoly on this expectation.
- In conclusion, the company said: Coca-Cola reiterates (its) product quality.
- (The CSE report levelled) unjustified baseless allegations on (Coke's) reputation.
- We (Coca-Cola India) follow identical worldwide protocols.
- Our position will be vindicated.
- We welcome debate on improving norms for potable water.
- Will work towards rebuilding consumer trust and confidence.
- The motivated report will be duly discarded.'

FICCI's presentation against the CSE's report was very comprehensive. Its 'damage assessment' highlighted several points :

- The serious health debate sweeping the country
- Questioned India's ability to manage its phyto-sanitary regulations before the global community
- Claimed that it projected a poor image of India's agriculture and food processing industry which is poised to target a leadership position in the world market
- Focussed on the fact that the finding could be exploited in trade negotiations affecting the country's export interest
- Argued that the global media coverage affected India's image with insinuations about its competence, skills and knowledge of the country's vast pool of scientific resources in knowledge

base, in as much as a country's well-established standards-setting systems
- Claimed it seriously affected both the bottled water/soft drink industry and all connected and costing the national exchequer a lot of revenues in levies and taxes.

FICCI said it was concerned about the 'sudden inclination towards adopting EU norms. We fail to understand the logic'. It felt the government reacted to the NGO report without making any attempt to verify their capabilities and effectiveness of testing procedures at such minute levels. The industry body was concerned that 'based on the benchmark used by the NGO, the (health ministry's) draft notification proposes arbitrary standards contrary to and deviating from any accepted international norms which are based on extensive research and data monitoring. The proposed new norms are devoid of any attempt to study the present system of standard setting and limit fixing procedures. The impact is far reaching, affects the very sensitive area of agriculture and food. India's strength in this area is well acknowledged. Developed countries try to create technical barriers to trade – standards are a major ploy. EU drinking water norms are not health based and, in any case, these standards are not applicable to finished products anywhere in the world, including the EU. The products are safe and well within Codex/WHO norms, which is the referral norm under WTO and also the ones India is gradually adopting. The fact is even if the NGO's results are taken as correct, our products are safe.' Singing the tune of the manufacturers (both Coke and Pepsi are members of FICCI), the presentation said there was no scientific basis for setting a total limit on pesticides in finished product. Each pesticide has its inherent toxicological and chemical properties. It would not react in the same manner as other pesticides. This was also taken into consideration when WHO, USEPA and Australia, set their drinking water limits for individual chemical. FICCI submitted that the application of pesticides limits based on EU drinking water norms to ready-to-serve beverages, was unscientific and arbitrary. The EU, WHO and the US do not apply drinking water pesticide residue standards to finished beverages, it argued. To follow such a practice in India would be unprecedented and contrary to international norms. Most juices, ready-to-drink teas, and sugar-sweetened finished beverages would not be able to meet the EU water standard even in Europe. The proposed heavy metal limits in finished beverages and juices are not consistent in all cases with international norms for beverages. Finally, FICCI told JPC that it should reject the NGO report and it should prescribe guidelines within which concerns for public health could be raised. 'Consumer health and safety concerns can be adequately addressed by fixing and enforcing limits for primary agricultural commodities and water as per the international practice. Food standards should be harmonised over time with Codex as per national policy. The new packaged drinking water norms should be cancelled and new norms which are in harmonisation with WHO/ Codex be adopted. The analytical methods should be standardised and prescribed for undertaking testing by appointing an expert committee for this purpose.' FICCI's observations and recommendations were 'too stereotyped' and an orchestration of the position taken by the two cola giants to deserve a special attention from most JPC members. However, the campaign did help in widening the scope of the pesticides controversy, beyond water and soft drinks, to cover fruits, vegetables, juices, tea and coffee. In the end, it did not seem to achieve much, except widen the rift between the cola giants, especially the more vulnerable Coke, and the NGOs and their support base. The direct attack on CSE did not go down well with other high-profile NGOs and MNC-bashers; thereby clearing the path for more fusillades from these powerful social service organisations in the near future.

The Lok Sabha Secretariat's *Report of Joint Committee on Pesticide Residues in and Safety Standards for Soft Drinks, Fruit Juice and Other Beverages*, 13th Lok Sabha, New Delhi, January 2004, Magha 1925 (Saka) is frequently referred to in this chapter.

Chapter 11

WATER THIEF

This chapter mainly draws on information provided by the INTACH Reports, The Lok Sabha Secretariat, *Report of Joint Committee on Pesticide Residues in and Safety Standards for Soft Drinks, Fruit Juice and Other Beverages*, 13th Lok Sabha, New Delhi, January 2004, Magha 1925 (Saka), BBC, Radio 4, 'Face the Facts', 25 July 2003, 12.30 p.m, [http://www.elaw.org/resources/text.asp?id=2360], 'Testing times for cola firms', *Frontline*, Vol. 20, Issue 17, August 16–29 2003,

'Toxins as manure', *Frontline,* Vol. 22, Issue 9, 23 April–6 May 2005, 'Clean chit to Plachimada plant', *The Hindu,* 30 September 2003, 'Coca-Cola's Kinley plant in Kerala hit by agitation', and *The Hindu Business Line,* 19 March 2004.

Chapter 12

PLACHIMADA GOES GLOBAL

Anita Roddick's website that contributed immensely to generating awareness is referred to in this chapter along with articles like 'Who guards the guardians?', *Economist,* 18 September 2003, 'Coca-Cola in India accused of leaving farms parched and land poisoned', *The Guardian,* 25 July 2003, 'Coca-Cola plant must stop draining water', *The Guardian,* 19 December 2003, 'Coke adds life?', *The Independent,* 25 July 2003, 'Conference asks soft drink MNCs to end water exploitation', *The Hindu,* 22 January 2004, 'Water not a private property', *The Hindu,* 24 January 2004, 'Anthony urged not to support Coca-Cola', *The Hindu,* 29 January 2004 and 'Two-faced capitalism – The future of corporate social responsi-bility', *Economist,* 22 January 2004.

Chapter 13

NOT THE REAL THING

This chapter refers to the following articles: 'Things go bitter with Coke', *The Observer,* 18 April 2004, 'Don't drink the water', *The Observer,* 18 April 2004 and 'Things get worse with Coke', *The Guardian,* 20 March 2004. The Annual Report of the Coca-Cola Company, 2002 and its website [http://company.monsterindia.com/cokein] also provide useful details.

POSTSCRIPT

The media report referred to on p.222 is 'Coke may hive off bottling business', *The Times of India,* 25 June 2004. HCCB's Annual Reports, 2003, 2004, 2005 and media reports following Isdell's farewell visit to India in 2008 proved helpful.

Index

PART I

Organizations/Institutions/Companies

PART II

Names of Places

Fig. 1: *Corporate Structure*

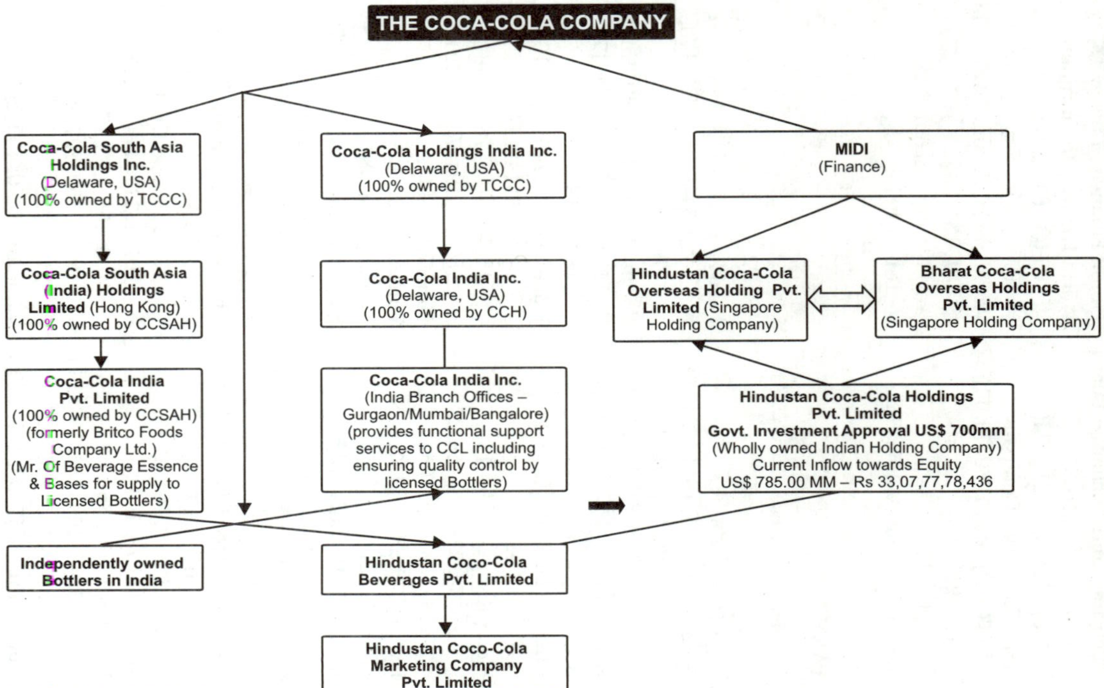

Source: TCCC Annual Report–2001

Fig. 2: *TCCC and HCCB relationship*

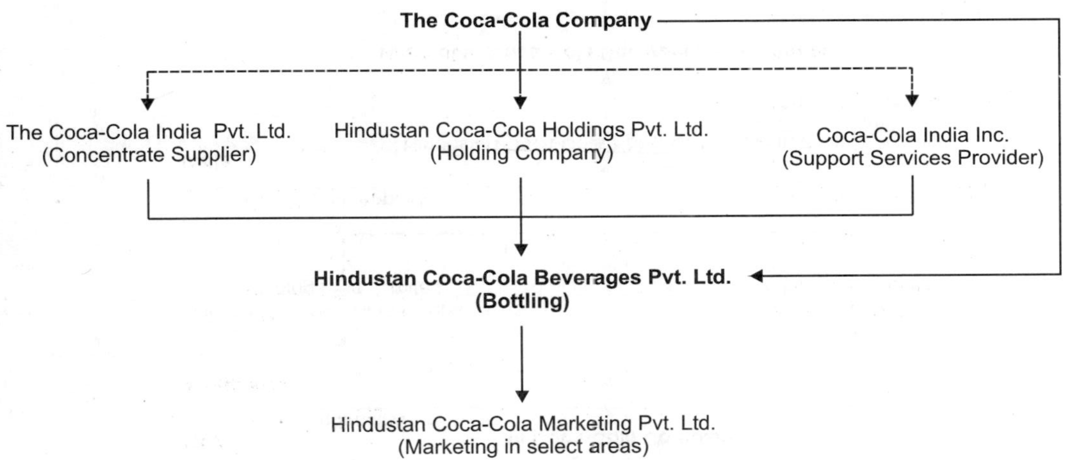

Source: TCCC Annual Report–2001

Fig. 3: *Ownership Structure*

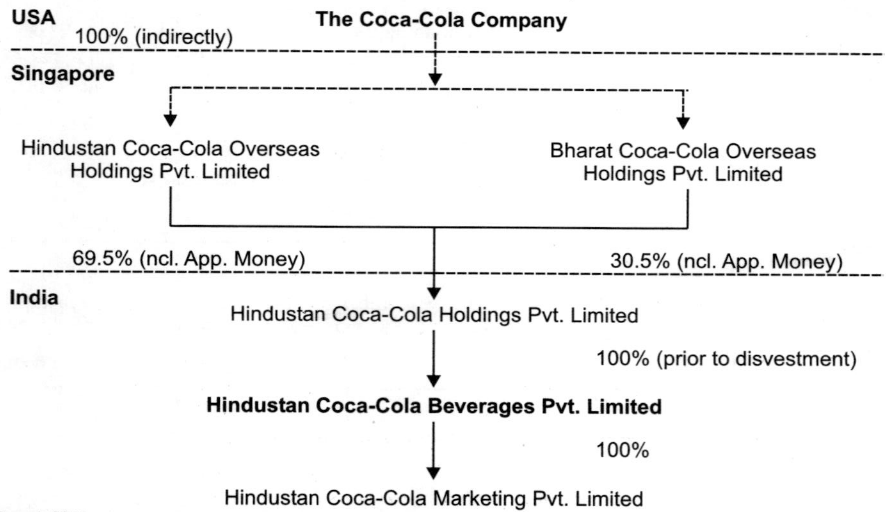

Source: TCCC Annual Report–2001